The English Mastiff
Owner's Manual

English Mastiff care, personality, grooming, health, costs and feeding all included

By
Harry Holstone

Dog lover and Mastiff Owner

Published by: IMB Publishing

Table of Contents

Table of Contents

Table of Contents

Foreword

Dogs are wonderful creatures. They are easily the best 'stress busters' that we could ask for. One thing that every dog lover would agree with is that they can be there for you always, unconditionally. So, it is every dog owner's responsibility to make sure that all the needs of the dog are fulfilled. The first step towards this is to ensure that you know everything that is required for the proper care of your beloved furry friend.

There are several dog breeds that require a great deal of care. These rare breeds are often brought to the rest of the world from a rather specific type of habitat. So, they need special conditions and special care so that they grow to be healthy and content. You definitely do not want to see your wonderful little pet moping around the house, almost seeming lazy and unhappy!

With breeds like the Mastiffs, the owners must be very well equipped to bring the dog home. These breeds are very powerful and can get behaviorally violent if they are not taken care of properly. As the owner, you must know how to train your Mastiff and help him become a social beast. If you fail to do that, you will be putting yourself and also your guests at a great risk. To begin with, Mastiffs are quite intimidating, given their size and their reputation. However, with the right owner, a Mastiff can be the most pleasurable pet to have at home.

If you are reading this book, they you either have a Mastiff at home or you are contemplating on bringing a Mastiff home. I really hope that you are the latter as this book will help you understand, whether or not the Mastiff is the right breed for you.

With the information that is provided in this book, you will be able to answer the three most common concerns of a pet owner:

a) Is it safe to have a certain breed at home?
b) What does the daily care for a certain breed include?
c) Am I financially and emotionally equipped to keep a breed content?

Important to mention

Please understand that much of the content written in this book can be applied to EVERY dog, because when it comes right down to it, a dog is a dog no matter what size, shape, color, price tag or fancy hybrid name we humans might attribute to them.

Every dog has a uniquely wonderful set of gifts to share with their human counterparts, if only us humans would listen.

They "tell" us when they are unhappy, when they are bored, when they are under-exercised, yet often we do not pay attention, or we just think they are being badly behaved.

Many humans today are deciding to have dogs, instead of children, and then attempting to manipulate their dogs into being small (or large) fur children. This is having a seriously detrimental effect upon the health and behavior of our canine companions.

In order to be the best guardians for our dogs, we humans need to have a better understanding of what our dogs need from us, rather than what we need from them, so that they can live in safety and harmony within our human environment. Sadly, many of us humans are not well equipped to give our dogs what they really need and that is why there are so many homeless, abandoned and frustrated dogs.
A professional dog whisperer is always challenged with the task of finding amicable solutions for canine/human relationships that have gone bad, once the humans understand what needs to be

changed, almost every stressful canine/human relationship can be turned into a happy, forever after.

The sad part is that many humans are simply not willing to do the work and devote the time necessary to ensuring that their dog's needs are met. Almost all canine problems are a direct result of ignorance or unwillingness on the part of the canine guardian to learn what the dog truly needs. Forget about the breed for the moment, because what the dog needs to be a happy and well-balanced family member has nothing to do with size, shape, color or breed.

First and foremost, our dogs need to be respected for their unique canine qualities. For millennia, dog has been considered *"Man's best friend"*, and in today's society, when we want to do the best by our canine companions and create a harmonious relationship, we humans need to spend more time receiving the proper training so that we humans can learn how Man can be dog's best friend.

Any dog can be "Man's best friend" providing that the human guardian gains the knowledge they need in order to create a happy environment for the dog.

If the human treats the dog well and understands what the dog needs, the dog will be happy and the owner will be happy. This applies to any dog. While basic training techniques apply to every dog, every dog and every human/dog relationship will be unique.

For this reason, when referring to daily feeding, care, house training, behavioral training, socializing, etc., these chapters are not written to apply specifically to the a certain breed, as this information can be applied equally successfully to any dog.

It is absolutely true that *"With the proper training, Man can learn to be dog's best friend."*

I hope that you enjoy reading this book as much as I enjoyed writing it.

Chapter 1: Introduction

The English Mastiff is often known as the "Gentle Giant". It is his calm and docile demeanor that has earned him this title. For those who are looking for a great companion who also doubles as a reliable watchdog, the English Mastiff is the perfect choice. The first thing you will notice about an English Mastiff is his size. These dogs are huge and can be quite a challenge for even a relatively large person to handle. However, his calm nature comes as a blessing to most English Mastiff owners who are initially worried about bringing home a dog as large as the English Mastiff.

The English Mastiff is a really ancient dog breed. This breed is known particularly for its large head, folded skin, intimidating size and a very interesting personality. While these dogs look like rather sloppy and lazy large fellows, do not be deceived by what is on the outside. The English Mastiff can be very powerful and is also quite ferocious when someone rubs him off wrongly! In fact, for several years, the English Mastiff was used as a hunting dog and a war dog.

Today, after being domesticated thoroughly, you will see that an English Mastiff is not particularly fond of hunting. He would prefer to just laze or lounge around and be on his toes only when something grabs his attention. You will be surprised at his agility and his state of alertness when something even as tiny as a mouse catches his attention. He has the ability to switch from a passive mode to a complete action mode within seconds!

The best thing about the English Mastiff is that it is a complete family dog. They are known for their strong protective instincts. These dogs will go out of their way to make sure that their family is safe. Of course, this also means that they love hanging around with members of their family. If you have an English Mastiff at home, you must make sure that there is someone with him, as much as possible. They can get really upset and sad if they are made to spend long hours without the company of their family.

For those who have owned or interacted with English Mastiffs, it is common knowledge that he is not a territorial dog per say. While they like to know that they have a territory of their own, they are not very protective about the property that they live in. Instead they will focus all their protective instincts towards their family.

The most interesting quality of an English Mastiff is that he is instinctively well behaved. These dogs are selfdom noisy and difficult to keep at home. All you need to do is ensure that your English Mastiff is well bred and really cared for. After that, proper socializing is good enough to have a dog who knows how he should behave around people. These dogs have the unique ability of gauging the difference between a threat and a non theat. That makes them all the more easy to have in your home. He will ensure that he does not alert you or bark without any reason.

With the English Mastiff, you will see a rather evident change in pace as he grows up. As puppies, English Mastiffs are highly active and rowdy. You will see that they love to jump, run about and even fall! However, as they grow up, they will become more reserved and will seem rather slow. Of course, their size makes them want to simply lounge around and relax. But, that does not mean that they have no power. If they are disturbed, they will attack with all their might.

Although the English Mastiff is not aggressive without reason, they are known to be quite dangerous when they are faced with any hazard to themselves or their family. Additionally, the sheer size of this breed acts a weapon of destruction. English Mastiffs love people and they tend to get jumpy and excited when they meet new people. So, you must pay a lot of attention to training them to stay down, heel and not jump upon people. Not many are strong enough to withstand the weight of these gentle giants.

These big guys, sadly, are unaware of their size! All they realize is that they love to snuggle up to their human friends or just sprawl around on the floor or the furniture. If your English Mastiff has learnt to snuggle up with you at night, make sure you get a bed that is large enough. If he doesn't find any space around you, he will make himself comfortable ON you! Now, that is something that we definitely do not want.

Despite the belief that the English Mastiff is dangerous, the most common sights are children and English Mastiffs playing quite happily. You will see that kids often make their English Mastiffs comfortable backrests as they complete their homework or read a book. These dogs can be very patient and will not mind being used as a little couch for the kids.

The only important thing with an English Mastiff is his upbringing. If you are able to get him to socialize and be around people from his puppy years, you can be sure that he will be very calm and gentle as he grows up. These dogs are perfect for almost anyone who is willing to spare time and put in some effort to ensure that their pet is happy.

Chapter 2: Characteristics of an English Mastiff

The English Mastiff is one of the most recognizable breeds of dogs. It has physical characteristics that are rather unique to the breed and, hence, it is quite easy for you to pick your English Mastiff. There are certain physical characteristics that you must look out for when you are bringing home an English Mastiff.

According to the Federation Cynologique Internationale, the English Mastiff is meant to be a guard dog and a defense dog. He is a breed that is par excellence. Despite the great size, this is a majestic beast is gifted with the mental balance to be docile and protective at the same time. These dogs are one of the best protectors of people as well a property. The FCI describes the English Mastiff as a brachymorph. This means that his trunk is longer that his height. However, the proportion of the physique of this breed is quite harmonious. Even the profile of this gorgeous beast is quite proportionate and visually pleasant.

The most obvious physical feature of the English Mastiff is his head. The large head of the Mastiff is known for the characteristic black mask. Usually, irrespective of the color of your English Mastiff, the muzzle and the area between his eyes have a very obvious black fur covering. This highlights the squarish and blunt shape of his rather large muzzle. The ears of the English Mastiff are also always black in color.

There is only one word that describes an English Mastiff aptly and the word is 'massive'. This dog has a stocky body, a large head and really huge bones. Usually, an English Mastiff would weigh about 150 pounds or about 70 kilos. The current Guinness

15

record for size is held by an English Mastiff named Zorba. Now, this beautiful brown Mastiff weighed about 156 kilos. Although since 2000, the Guinness book of world records stopped taking entries for largest and heaviest animals, I stated the example of Zorba to give you an idea about how large these babies can get!

The interesting thing about the English Mastiff is that he looks really bulky and huge. However, he is not the tallest amongst the Giant dog breeds. Still, the English Mastiff is considered to be the largest Mastiff, in terms of his mass. When he is fully grown he can get really heavy! Of course, there is one really nice thing about the English Mastiff. He retains his puppyhood for a long time! This means he is not completely mature unless he is three years old. Of course, the English Mastiff does attain his complete height by the time he is one year old. However, he takes three long years to get to his full weight.

1. Decoding the Coat

Now, the coat of your English Mastiff is a very important thing. It is the mark of a healthy dog. It is also a great quality in the English Mastiff as it determines the grooming needs of your dog. The coat of the English Mastiff is usually hard, dense, stiff and short. The fur is of uniform length all over the body. So it is much easier to groom in comparison to other dogs. All you need to do is give your Mastiff a good wash and he is good to go. Of course, he will need other kinds of grooming which we will get to in the following chapters.

Do Mastiffs shed a lot of fur? Well not really. However, there are seasonal woes that you must prepare yourself for. In the spring and fall seasons, your English Mastiff will leave behind traces of hair wherever he rests (or sprawls!). Of course, there is nothing that cannot be cured with a little bit of brushing. During these seasons, all you need to do is regularly brush off the loose hairs so that your home is fur- free. You can also use a shedding blade along with a sisal mitt to remove the dead hair from the surface.

The coat colors for this breed are very limited. You will mostly find English Mastiffs that are apricot in color. Brindling is common with the English Mastiff. Brindling refers to lines or marking on the coat of the dog or on a part of the coat. The colors of the brindles range from apricot, black to yellow.

2. Breed Standards

The characteristics of an English Mastiff are very specific. Although to most of us, just the above features are good enough to make a loving pet at home, there are some other pet owners who are very interested in showing their English Mastiffs. If you are one of them, they you must be aware of certain breed standards that will qualify your English Mastiff for showing.

These standards have been set by the Federation Cynologique International which is a federation o kennel clubs. This federation is based in Thiun, Belgium. When the name of the federation is translated into English it becomes the World Canine Organization. Of course, this name is not commonly used and most people refer to these guidelines as the FCI guidelines.

The objective of the FCI is to promote the breeding of purebred dogs like the English Mastiff. They have set basic standards to ensure that breeders are producing puppies that have complete functional health. It is also important for the physical features of a dog to match the recommended characteristics for the breed to ensure that the dogs are able to accomplish functions that are expected of the certain breed. For instance, an English Mastiff who is not as powerful as recommended by the standards will not be able to play the role of a guard dog as well as a dog that is really up to all the mentioned standards.

The FCI also encourages the exchange of information about canines between various member countries. This helps them initiate organization of various breed exhibitions across the globe. It also provides them with opportunities to understand the requirements to produce healthy specimens.

The FCI standards recommended for the English Mastiff are as follows:

General Appearance: An English Mastiff must appear massive and heavy. They are thick set and are of great size. The length of the body must be greater than the height at the withers. The withers refer to the ridge-like formation that you will see at the point where the shoulder blades of the English Mastiff meet.

The Body: The body of an English Mastiff is all about power and muscularity. Their body is long and deep. The broad shoulders and the proportionate build of the English Mastiff is unique to this breed. The muscularity of the back and the loins is very important for a Mastiff. For females the back is flat while the males have a slightly curved back. The depth of the flanks is also a conspicuous feature of the English Mastiff's body.

The ribs have a well defined arch. The shoulders are very heavily muscled and are placed obliquely. The chest of the English Mastiff should look like it is being help up majestically. For this, the ideal proportion of the chest to the shoulder height is 1:3.

Temperament: The English Mastiff must be loyal and calm. He must never bite without reason or even be overly aggressive. The primary function of an English Mastiff is that of a protector. He must be able to defend the property that he is responsible for and also take care of the inhabitants of the property. As a result, the English Mastiff must be extremely steady and loyal. He must also have a noble and majestic demeanor. The body language of the English Mastiff should be that of a very vigilant and intelligent dog, rather than sloppy and lazy.

Head and Skull: The most striking quality of an English Mastiff is the size of his head. It is enormous! All the facial muscles including the muscles in the cheeks and the temples are highly developed. You can see an arch across the skull. It looks like a curve that is visible in the form of a curve at the centre of the forehead. The skin on the head in not loose except near the mouth

18

where it forms the trademark dewlap. However, you can see wrinkles in the forehead when the dog is in a state of excitement.

The head of an English Mastiff has a very square appearance. No matter what side you look at the head from, it should appear boxy and rectangular. Width is a matter of great concern when you think of the head of an English Mastiff. From every angle the head must appear wide and large.

The brows of the English Mastiff are gorgeous. They are excellently developed and the furrow in the front is well visible. Although the brows are not very high raised, they do attract a great deal of attention.

The nose of the English Mastiff is broad. When you look from the front, the nostrils look really wide. When you view the Mastiff from the side, the nose has a very flat appearance.

The Muzzle: The muzzle is blunt and short. The area just below the eyes is quite broad. When you look at the width of the muzzle it remains almost parallel till the end of the nose. The muzzle of the English Mastiff is truncated. This means that the muzzle is placed at an exact right angle with the line of the face. Also the point of the nose until the under jaw has a pronounced depth.

The Lips: The lips of the English Mastiff are a very important feature. The distinct V shape that is formed at the junction of the upper lips is very important for a show English Mastiff. The upper lips are very thick and fleshy. The upper lips of the English Mastiff form the lower profile of the muzzle. The lowest part of the muzzle is that at the corner of the lips where you can see the mucous membrane quite evidently. You can actually draw a straight line from this lowest point to the outer corner of the eye of an English Mastiff giving the face a trademark geometric appearance.

The Jaws: As I mentioned before, the breed standards have been established in order to have fully functioning specimen. Now, if the English Mastiff is meant to be a protector, his jaws must be powerful enough to do that. The jaws of the English Mastiff are extremely powerful in appearance. They have very strong bones that have perfectly fitted dental arches. The lower jaw is always well developed in the width.

The Eyes: The eyes of an English Mastiff are very well placed. They are completely forward facing and are placed apart from one another. The eyes are tiny and the space between the eyes is equal to the width of two eyes. There is no abrupt stop between the eyes, although it is well defined. The eyes are usually hazel brown in color and can come in various shades of this color. Of course, the darker the eyes, the better it is.

The Ears: The ears are droopy when your puppy is brought home. However, some dog owners prefer to have the ears cropped off the make the English Mastiff look more alert and ferocious. In comparison with the rest of the body, the ears are rather small, even when they are not cropped. They have a triangular shape and are flat in their appearance. These ears are held very close to the cheek bone when they are flappy. In case of an English Mastiff with cropped ears, they will form a perfect equilateral triangle.

The Mouth: The teeth are flawlessly white and are quite strongly developed. The English Mastiff has a scissor bite dentition is one in which the upper incisors of the English Mastiff are very closely placed over the lower incisors. However, the projection is not so much that the teeth become visible even when the mouth of the Mastiff is shut.

The Neck: The Neck of the English Mastiff is slightly arched. It is short in length. Usually, the length of the next is about 28% of the height at the shoulder blades. The neck is very well muscled and has a conical shape. It is also blunt in appearance. When you measure the circumference of the neck at different levels, you will notice that at mid length, the circumference of the neck is $1/8^{th}$ the size of the height at withers.

The Forequarters: When compared to the size of the body of your English Mastiff, the forelegs must look strong and well balanced to take the weight of this huge canine. The most important part of the forelegs is the area from the ground to the elbow. When you look at this part from the side or from the front, it should look completely vertical. The bone structure should be well developed and must appear extremely strong. The bones of the legs are large and the pasterns are square.

Needless to say, the shoulders make for a very important part of the English Mastiff's body. When measured from a vertical place, the shoulders are placed at a 50 or 60 degree angle. The muscles in the shoulder are very strong and are highly developed. The definition of the shoulder muscles is also a very important feature of the English Mastiff.

The front feet are quite large and have toes that are very close knit. The pads below the feet are firm and hard. The pigmentation of the pads is also very prominent and is a contrast to the skin tone of the English Mastiff. The nails are also very well defined. They are dark, curved and very strong.

The Hindquarters: Just like the forelegs, even the hind legs are judged as per their ability to balance the entire massive structure of the dog. For this they must look super sturdy and powerful. The hind legs have another important role to play. They must provide the right amount of propulsion to enable the dog to run and chase.

The hind quarters are very strong and are extremely muscular. What makes the hindquarters look great is the formation of the second thigh. Usually the hock joint is slightly bent. When the English Mastiff is standing upright, the hind legs are set wide apart and are set squarely when the dog is standing straight.

Gait: The gait is a very important trait in every breed of dog. With a majestic breed like the English Mastiff, it is still more important as your dog must look like he is in complete control. As for the walking, the gait should be like a lion, quite feline, in fact. What this means is that the dog must be very light on his feet when he is walking. When he is trotting or pacing, he should resemble a bear. That means, even with the massive body, your English Mastiff must look agile and powerful. A goof trotting gait is one in which the hind quarter has ample thrust to push into the forequarters. Basically, he should have a very smooth take off. An English Mastiff will gallop very rarely. Pacing is accepted for this breed, but not too often.

The Tail: The tail of the English Mastiff is set high. The tail is long enough to reach the hocks. Sometimes, the tail may fall a little below the hock joint as well. It is acceptable. The tail has a typical tapering shape. It starts off quite thick at the roots and becomes thin towards the end. When the dog is relaxed, the tail may be hanging down straight. However, in a state of excitement, the tail must form a curve and must be pointed upwards.

Colors: The most common colors that are accepted as per the standards are fawn, apricot and brindled. The brindles on the fur are yellow, brown or apricot. The muzzle, ears and the nose must be black. The eyes have a dark black outline. Having excessive white color on the chest, feet and the body is not acceptable.

Size: The English Mastiff is a rather tall dog. The height is measured at the withers to determine the standards. In males, the height is between 76 to 91 cms while in the females, the height is between 70 cms to 85 cms. The dogs are heavy, as mentioned before.

3. Cropping the Ears of an English Mastiff

When we are discussing the physical traits of an English Mastiff, we must speak in more detail about cropping the ears of the dog. While several animal rights activists consider it an act of cruelty, there are many pet owners across the globe that opt for this cosmetic procedure to make their pets more aesthetic to look at. According to many breeders and pet owners, cropping is essential to give a breed it's distinct and trademark appearance. For instance, picture a Doberman without a cropped tail and ears. Now, it is your personal choice to have the ears of your English Mastiff cropped. However, if you do chose to do so, you must be aware of the procedure and its consequences to make the right decision.

Cropping through the ages

Cropping the ear has been a customary practice for an English Mastiff. Studies related to artworks that are thousands of years old, containing images of the English Mastiff show that the ears of the dog were cropped. In those days, the ears of the English Mastiff were cropped in order to make them suitable for fights. A hanging and flappy ear could be ripped off quite easily by an opponent, causing severe damage to the dog's health. Of course, the dog would be defeated in the fight, as well.

Today, cropping the ear is a completely cosmetic procedure. Pet owners who are interested in showing their English Mastiff opt for cropping. There are some arguments that cropping the ear is also done for health purposes. They believe that the ear that's cropped is less prone to infections and problems.

How does cropping change the appearance of the English Mastiff?

The only problem with the regular ears of an English Mastiff is that it makes the dog look rather lazy and slow. So, when these dogs are entered in shows, it is necessary to make them look alert. For this reason the ears of an English Mastiff are cropped. Additionally, the English Mastiff has certain functions that require him to look powerful. Picture a lazy looking dog guarding a ranch! When the ears are cropped, the English Mastiff looks less vulnerable and hence, keeps trespassers at bay.

Styles of ear cropping

Depending upon the size of the ear after it is cropped, there are two styles. This is common for any breed that requires cropping of the ears. The first style is known as the "pet" style. This is when the ear is completely cropped off. The second style is known as the "show style" where a little bit of the ear is left intact to give the ear an upright and alert position. You must always look for an experienced vet to help your Mastiff. Amateurs might give the dog an ugly triangular cut that just does not work for your dog in the actual market. Another thing that you must keep in mind is that there are chances of the cropped ears looking uneven although they are the same in terms of the measurement. This is because the texture of the pinnae might be different for each ear.

How the ears are cropped?

The ears are cropped surgically. Usually a brace is used to keep the ear standing upright so that the dog looks alert. These braces are made of cardboard and other similar materials to ensure that the ear is place while it is developing. It is recommended that the surgery is done when the English Mastiff is still a puppy. These are the developing years when the cartilage of the ear is still in its formative stage. So placing the brace will set the ear in place completely. The time frame that you have to get the ear cropped is rather small. Your English Mastiff must be old enough to take the surgical procedure. If the puppy is too delicate, you always run the risk of infections and also complications in the procedure. At the same time, the puppy must also be young enough so that the cartilage is not completely formed. The best time to get the ears of the English Mastiff cropped is between 6 and 12 weeks of age. It is ideal if your English Mastiff is 8 weeks old.

The amount of cartilage present in the ear does not change when you opt for cropping. When the puppies are born, there is a leathery flap that extends out. It is only this flap that gets cut in order to reduce the length of the English Mastiff's ears. If you make a short cut in the ear, the time taken for it to set and stand in an upright position is not much. On the other hand, if you are opting for the long cut, the procedure is a little more time consuming.

Cost

The cost of the crop depends entirely upon the breed of the dog. Another factor that determines the cost is the type of cropping that you opt for. In this case, the length of the crop and the amount of support that it requires to set in place comes into the picture. If you are opting for a special sow crop, be prepared to shell out more money. This type of cropping requires an expert. Your local vet will not be able to provide you with the precision that is required to have the ears cropped.

The cropping process is not complex. The surgery does not lead to any complications. However, it is the supplies, the anesthesia, the facilities and the expertise that you end up paying for. The cost of the ear crop will be anything between $200 and $500. That is between 100 to 250 pounds.

Remember, if you notice any infections; rush your English Mastiff to a doctor. You must also make sure you follow up with your vet on a regular basis.

Chapter 3: Summary of the Physical Characteristics

Weight in the Male-   115- 155 lbs/ 65- 75 kilos

Weight in the Female- 100-132 lbs / 50 to 60 kilos

Eye Color-   Different shades of brown

Life Span- 8 to 10 years

Attention Demand- High

Shedding of Fur – Seasonal, usually in spring and fall

Length of Fur- Short, not more that 1.5 cms

 Texture of Coat – Thick, stiff and smooth

Color- Apricot, fawn or brindled

Allergenic Property – Moderate

Grooming Needs- Moderate

Associations that recognize the breed- FCI, KC, AKC, ANKC, CKC, NZKC, UKC.

Prevalence of the Breed- Common

Banned in: The state of Iowa

Chapter 4: The English Mastiff and the American Mastiff

The purity of a breed is extremely important when you are interested in dogs like the English Mastiff. These breeds have been around for centuries and have been preserved by several breeders because of their interesting temperament and also their unique physical features. There are several pet owners who are, in fact, against creating new lines of dogs from ancient breeds like the English Mastiff. The American Mastiff is one such breed which received a lot of criticism from 'purist' breeders and dog owners. Nevertheless, this breed did receive many loving homes and has grown to become popular across the globe.

The American Mastiff and the English Mastiff are so similar in their appearance that it is difficult for a novice to really know what breed he is bringing home. If you are particular about the bringing home an English Mastiff, here are some differences that you must look out for.

Difference between the breeds

- **History of the Breeds:** The English Mastiff has a long and ancient history. These dogs were typically used as war dogs and were bred to be ferocious war dogs. We will discuss the history of the English Mastiff in greater detail in the following chapters. The American Mastiff is actually a descendant of the English Mastiff. This breed was created in Piketon Ohio about 25 years backs. That makes it a very recent breed. The American Mastiff was created by crossing an English Mastiff with an Anatolian Shepherd Dog.

- **Size**: To the normal eye, it does not seem like there is a size difference between an English and American Mastiff. These two breeds grow to almost the same height, which is an average 36 inches. However, they are very different in their mass. While the English Mastiff is a bulky and heavy dog who achieves a weight of close to 155 pounds / 75 kilos when he is fully grown, an American Mastiff reaches a maximum weight of about 140 pounds which is about 70 kilos.

- **Appearance**: The head is where the main difference between the two breeds lies. Both the dogs have large heads. However, with the American Mastiff, the head seems to be a little too large for his body. The muzzle of an American Mastiff is often shorter that the English Mastiff. The Muzzle of an American Mastiff is very similar the muzzle of a Great Dane. With the English Mastiff, the upper lip hangs considerably loosely over the lower lip. In case of the American Mastiff, the lips are a more tightly fitted.

- **Texture of the coat**: The coat on the English Mastiff is smoother in comparison to the American Mastiff. Both the dogs are short haired. Another difference that you must know with respect to the coat is the amount of shedding that occurs. An American Mastiff tends to shed more hair than the English Mastiff. So if you are a cleanliness junkie, you must opt for an English Mastiff.

- **Temperament**: A lot of English Mastiff lovers had an issue with the American Mastiff because they believed that mixing the blood of a Anatolian Shepherd Dog's blood in this line ruined the temperament that the English Mastiff is popular for. There are some rather noticeable differences between the temperaments of these two breeds. The English Mastiff is basically a guardian dog. This makes him very protective in nature and also quite fearless. The English Mastiff is a very obedient dog but, he can be quite dominant in some cases. He is also stubborn when it comes to the protection of his family and property. He is also alert and will spring into action when he perceives any danger.

The American Mastiff, on the other hand, is not much of a guardian. He is not as alert or intelligent as his parent breed. The American Mastiff is also known to be very scared of danger and sudden discomfort. However, he is even tempered, reserved and timid in his approach. An American Mastiff makes a great companion who is loyal and highly social. He is a calm dog who stays quite for the most part.

• **Life Expectancy**: An English Mastiff, like most giant dogs has a short life span. He has a life expectancy of about 8 to 10 years. On the other hand, the American Mastiff lives slightly longer than the English Mastiff for about 10 to 12 years.

• **Health**: The American Mastiff was created with the sole purpose of reducing the health problems in the English Mastiff. This was achieved and hence, the American Mastiff lives a healthier life than the English Mastiff. He is also lesser prone to "giant dog diseases" like hip dysplasia.

Similarities between the two breeds:

There are some obvious similarities between these two breeds. To begin with, one is the descendant of the other. So they are genetically quite similar.

The English Mastiff and the American Mastiff are quite easy to maintain. They do not shed their skin too much and require minimum grooming like simple brushing to keep them pleasant on the eyes. These dogs are also quite bulky, although the American Mastiff is significantly smaller than the English Mastiff.

Both the English Mastiff and the American Mastiff are considered to be working dogs. They are used as protectors my most owners. These dogs are also highly trainable, making it a pleasure to have them at home. They also love to play and hang around with their human companions.

When you are purchasing an English Mastiff puppy, which is rather expensive, be sure to ask the breeder for all the possible information to ensure that you are bringing the right breed home.

Chapter 5: History of the English Mastiff

The English Mastiff is an ancient dog breed. He has had a very transformative history in terms of his purpose and his temperament. Over the ages, man tried to retain the qualities of the English Mastiff that were best suited for his needs. Therefore, the dog became more timid over time and also became a versatile breed that could also make a great companion. The history of an English Mastiff is rather interesting to trace. We will start from the beginning and understand what this breed was really known for and what makes him the lovable mutt that he is today.

Prehistoric times

It is true that this breed was popular even in the pre—historic times. There is also ample proof to suggest that this is. Archaeologists have discovered several relics that carry images of dogs that look similar to the English Mastiff. These relics were made as early as 2200 BC. During those times, the Mastiffs had already gained popularity as working dogs and were used for several activities. Some even suggest that these dogs were highly misused as war dogs or fight dogs.

Some sculptures found in Assyria reveal that dogs that were similar to the English Mastiff were used in 650 BC as domestic dogs and also war dogs. There is no clarity on how these dogs were bred, however. The only thing that breeders and historians know for sure is that this breed originated in Central Asia. These dogs came to Britain when they were traded by the Phoenicians as early as 500 BC.

There are several theories associated with the origin of this dog. No one knows if these dogs were simply a miracle of nature or whether there was some genuine human effort that went into producing the breed. The only thing that we know for certain is that they were loved by the British who took interest in them because of their sheer size and the strength that they had. The history of the English Mastiff is rather dreadful as many dogs were sacrificed on the behest of sport and wars. Organized fights between animals were popular at that time and many indulged in it. Therefore people put different breeds of dogs and different animals against each other. The most common fights back then were between dogs and bears. So, many Mastiffs lost their lives because of the inhuman fancies of the people living in those times.

The Romans grew particularly fond of the English Mastiff. They thought that the breed was a perfect symbol for the Roman Empire which was at its peak at those times. Rome was also popular for their breeds of war and fight dogs. When Britain was under the rule of the Romans, several English Mastiffs were exported to Rome. These dogs were made to fight for their lives in order to survive amongst the Romans.

The Romans brought home several dogs from their expeditions across the globe. The English Mastiff was one of the most popular ones. They were able to fight against ferocious creatures like the African Lions. During those days, there were no laws to protect these animals, sadly. But, the one thing that is quite interesting is that the Romans had nothing but praise for the amazing Mastiffs. These dogs were actually symbols of great honor and status. Even today, the English Mastiff is considered a status symbol by many. His enormous structure and his whole appearance makes him look regal.

These dogs were trained by the Romans for was and to provide protection. They were given a very specific type of training that made them extremely ferocious and highly protective by nature. There are also tales of many Roman Mastiffs who were considered war heroes. One such Mastiff who gave up his life fighting for his master was Julius Caesar's favorite dog.

The fifteenth century

During these times there was great apathy in England. Most of the population was extremely poor. Contrasting their condition were the rich who enjoyed all the luxuries one could conceive at that time. The tax laws were unfair and the rich also used a lot of political and religious power to keep this difference intact. The mass did not even have proper food to eat. Their sole source of food was the meat that they obtained by hunting. Another issue was that most of the forest land belonged to the upper class. These people caught and released many animals into the jungles. Now these animals made very desirable sport but were not available to the poor. On the other hand, the rich just hunted them for fun. Eventually, the poor were unable to come to terms with the temptation to hunt these animals and get some food. They resorted to illegal hunting. Of course, the landowners considered this a menace and trained Mastiffs to solve the problem for them. These Mastiffs were trained to scare the hunters off the property that belonged to these landlords.

To accommodate the Mastiffs, a new law was made in England. The only dogs that were allowed in the property of these landlords were the Mastiffs. They were made mandatory as they were great at keeping illegal hunters at bay. During the 15th century, the Mastiff also gained popularity as a hunting dog that was trained to track down larger animals.

The modern Mastiff

The real 'modern Mastiff' came into being in the 20th century. During this time, there were very few of the original race that had survived and made it. In order to carry the bloodline forth, some people in England made a committed effort towards producing newer generations of the Mastiff. They wanted to ensure that the breed does not perish altogether. This is when a rebuilding program for the Mastiff began in England. The earliest experiments involved a mixture of the Mastiffs with giant dogs like the St. Bernard. The mixing was necessary to ensure that the puppies were healthy. The results that they got were quite good. Just before the Second World War began, the breed had been reinforced and was no longer under threat. During those times, dog shows that displayed very high quality English Mastiffs became popular. However, the good times did not last too long. When the war began, these dogs, especially the big ones were in threat once again. This is because these large dogs required a lot of food. But then, food was a luxury during those troubled times.

Post Second World War

When the Second World War ended, it was observed that most of the English Mastiff dogs had perished again. A meeting took place in London in 1946 that would change the fate of this breed yet again. Fifteen English Mastiff enthusiasts met in London. They were about to embark upon a journey that most breeders had given up on. They met to save this wonderful breed from becoming extinct.

These enthusiasts vowed to do everything in their power to bring back the breed of English Mastiffs. Their plan was to track down all the Mastiffs that were still alive in the country. Following this, they would try to ensure that all the puppies in a litter were born alive and maintained under healthy conditions. However, it was too late for them to execute the plan. Amongst the twenty odd dogs that were still alive, many were too old to reproduce. One famous incident that took place back then was the birth of three litters of eighteen puppies, fathered by an English Mastiff named Tarsus. Sadly, only one of them survived! This heralded the doom of this breed. By 1947, only seven English Mastiffs were alive in England.

The only hope was a visit to the United States where these breeders hoped to find healthier dogs. Sadly, the quality of the dogs in the USA was also very poor. As a result, no dog was brought back to England.

In 1948, there seemed some hope for this gentle giant. Two puppies were sent to England from the District of Colombia. These puppies were promising and became the foundation for all the Mastiffs that we see today. By 1949, the numbers had increased to 15 and by 1950, there were close to 50 Mastiffs in England. In order to achieve these numbers, several breeds that had similar backgrounds and histories were put to use. Breeds like the St. Bernard, the Bull Mastiff and the Great Dance were used as they were believed to be closely related to the English Mastiff.

There were other breeds like the Boxer, the Rottweiler, the Bloodhound and the English Bull dog that had descended from the Molossus breed of dogs. This mixing led to several types of Mastiffs that we know of today. Thankfully, these breeds are still going strong. Some common Mastiffs that are seen today are the Spanish Mastiff, the Pyrenean Mastiff and the Neapolitan Mastiff. The English Mastiff, however is considered to be the main breed and is usually just referred to as "the Mastiff".

Today , the English Mastiff is mostly a family dog. He is not meant for violence of any sort. He makes a great watchdog who loves to keep an eye on his home. He has the tact of convincing trespassers that they are not welcome without invitation. Although these dogs are extremely gentle, they will attack when they feel like their safety is being compromised.

As a traditional practice, English Mastiffs continue to be used as watchdogs outside pubs in England. These dogs are gentle but their size and the low pitched, but loud bark is good enough to prevent anyone from getting too close or trying to challenge his intentions.

It is difficult to say that the English Mastiff is a popular breed. Considering that there are only about 1000 individuals in the UK and about the same number in the west, it is a less prevalent breed world over. In comparison to most breeds this is a small number. In countries like Norway, there are less than 100 English Mastiffs.

With more understanding of dealing with giant breeds like the English Mastiff, it is possible that there will be many more dogs globally. Their increasing popularity as show dogs also makes the future promising for the English Mastiffs.

Chapter 6: Personality of the English Mastiff

Knowing the personality of a certain breed is helpful in two ways: First, you understand whether the dog that you are planning to bring home is suitable for your family and home environment. Second, it also helps you be prepared to deal with certain requirements of breeds like the English Mastiff.

Over the years, dog like the English Mastiff has undergone a lot of changes in terms of his temperament. It is a wonder that this dog is perceived as a cuddly companion today. A few centuries ago, he would have probably been the last thing you want lying on your sofa! As the Mastiff breed was crossed with other giant breeds to increase the numbers, they underwent a drastic change in their personality. Today the temperament that breeders have achieved is perfect to make him the best companion and watchdog that you can imagine. Breeders have tried their best to maintain this temperament for the breed as it made the functionality of the breed better. So, when you are bringing home an English Mastiff, you must be prepared for a dog who simple loves to be around you, a dog who doesn't know how big he is and a dog who will, literally, slobber you with love. Here are some traits that are unique to the English Mastiff:

1. The Peaceful Beast

The English Mastiff looks like a ferocious beast, especially when his ears have been cropped off. He also has the reputation of being a dog that was used in fights and hunts. Therefore, many believe that the English Mastiff is a very ferocious animal to bring home.

The truth is quite contrary and the English Mastiff is really one of the gentlest beasts you could ever think of. Yes, they are protective and can get aggressive when they see any signs of danger. However, an English Mastiff will never attack anyone without any reason. They will   not even show traces of irritation even when they are amongst lot of people, if you have trained them to be social.

Socializing an English Mastiff is the first step towards ensuring that he behaves well with your guests and visitors. There are several owners who believe that making an English Mastiff social will reduce his capacity as a good guard dog. This is completely false as the English Mastiff is a highly sensitive creature. He will sense the difference between an individual who is trespassing and an individual who is your friend or acquaintance in a jiffy if he is adequately socialized.

Remember, the English Mastiff is a highly vigilant fellow. So he will make it a point to observe everything about strangers and other unwanted visitors thoroughly before he decides to attack.

2. Loyal Guardian

Many breeders will tell you that the English Mastiff is not a loyal dog. Do not take their word for it. As I mentioned before, ancient owners of this breed believed that they had to cut the toes off to ensure that the dog does not wander away. You, however, need to do no such thing. An English Mastiff is so protective of the people that he lives with; he will take it as his personal responsibility to keep them safe. So, he will never wander away from your home

Like all large dogs, the English Mastiffs are also pets who require a lot of attention from the owners. So, they get quite attached to the people who take care of them. This trait has been a part of their lives for centuries now and cannot be changed very easily. In fact, if you decide to move or shift, your English Mastiff might even resist it because of the love that he develops for his home. Keeping all this in mind, there is no need to doubt the loyalty of you English Mastiff.

The English Mastiff's world revolves around his master. The person, who is in charge of him, means the world to an English Mastiff. If you gave the English Mastiff a choice, he would pick spending time with his master over anything else. This also shows that the English Mastiff seeks some sort of companionship. However, he does prefer having his master around in comparison to having another canine or animal companion.

Many people still view the English Mastiff as a status symbol and will just keep him tied up in the yard. If you intend to do the same, then do not bring home an English Mastiff. He will punish you for negligence, alright! Of course, he will not pounce on your or try to harm you, he will just dig up massive holes around his resting area in the yard. The most difficult thing to manage is a bored English Mastiff. He will try to explore whatever is around him and will call out to you in scary, low pitched barks! If you are up for dealing with that, you may consider ignoring your English Mastiff.

The English Mastiff has unique ways of showing his love for you. When you are home, he will follow you around. He loves to be a part of your daily life and will be inquisitive about what you are doing. Of course, he also wants you to play with him! So, if you are taking the day off and just watching a couple of movies and lounging around, your English Mastiff will wait by your feet eager to play or go out for a stroll when you decide to get off that couch. He will watch you closely and will get excited at your every second move.

So, you see, no matter what anyone tells you, know that your English Mastiff is loyal to a fault. All you need to do to gain his trust is shower him with some kind words and he will remain loyal for a lifetime! Considering his size and his appearance, the English Mastiff does seem like a rather softie from within, doesn't he?

3. Pecking Order

The English Mastiff is known for his unique soft mouth quality. This gives him the ability to carry delicate and small creatures like squirrels in his mouth without causing them any damage. So if you have tiny people or creatures in your home, danger from the English Mastiff is the least of your concerns. He will never attack or be aggressive towards resident pets, if any. He will also adjust to new pets if introduced correctly. In totality, the English Mastiff is compatible with most people and animals in your home, as long as they are not strangers who are a threat.

Like any pet that you would bring home, you must also consider the pecking order of the English Mastiff. Sure, he is a gentle dog who is seldom aggressive. However, you must never underestimate the primeval instincts of any pet that you bring home. Yes, there are several people who have other pets and also children at home and still manage to keep the English Mastiff. But, it does take a good understanding of the dog's psychology to make this happen. If you are not sure of how to handle your children and the English Mastiff or other pets and the English Mastiff, here are a few tips.

To begin with, remember that it is never ever a good idea to have a child alone with a dog, the English Mastiff or any other breed.

They are both innocent and highly rely upon instincts. So, make sure you have some supervision when the English Mastiff and a baby are interacting with one another. The English Mastiff is very tolerant towards children and makes a great couch and backrest for the kids. However, that does not mean that he is meant to entertain your child. He will not be too pleased if your child constantly teases or bothers the dog. Remember, the English Mastiff is programmed to attack when threatened. Therefore, if there is a kid in the picture, you should always make the child aware of the fact that the dog is not a toy.

The English Mastiff is a dog that requires a commanding master, whether it is an adult or a child. Now, an English Mastiff is pretty gentle towards human children and will never hurt them on purpose. However, the size of the English Mastiff is also a threat to the well being of a child. Sometimes, in their excitement, English Mastiffs may knock over and even step on children and hence harm the child. So, it is best that you are around when your child is with the Mastiff.

When it comes to other pets, the English Mastiff is tolerant towards them as long as he gets to be the boss. If you have another dog which is an alpha by nature, you must reconsider bringing home an English Mastiff. They never get along with another animal who wants mastery over their territory. For instance, if you have two English Mastiffs of the same gender in your household, you must consider separating them and reducing the severity of the disagreements that they might have. If you have a female and a male, on the other hand, the male will allow himself to be subdued while the female takes over. There are some cases when the female and male will also fight for an alpha position. So, if you are housing English Mastiffs at home, it is best that you keep them away from each other.

With smaller animals, you are just putting them at risk with an English Mastiff. These dogs love to chase creatures that are smaller than them. Of course, you can control the interactions and supervise, but you can never control the outcome of unsupervised interactions between your English Mastiff and the other smaller animals that you have at home.

In conclusion, the English Mastiff's pecking order is as follows:

1.   Kids
2.   Other dogs
3.   Smaller animals like cats

That being said, try to avoid unsupervised interactions at all times.

4. Highly Energetic

An English Mastiff has loads of energy. Most often, they like to let this energy out by chasing. His favorite chasing targets are cyclists and vehicles. English Mastiffs also enjoy chasing a small and fast animal like a cat or rabbit. This makes it important for the owners to be very careful to ensure that the English Mastiff does not cause any damage to other animals and people. He must also be protected as chasing vehicles and cycles might lead to severe accidents.

An English Mastiff must be trained to be obedient to avoid bad behavior. Training does not involve punishing or reprimanding your dog for bad behavior. The best thing to do with an English Mastiff is to appreciate him when he behaves in a manner that is acceptable to you. They are very quick to learn the difference between what is socially acceptable and what is not.

As the owner, you must be in charge at all times. It best if there is one consistent master who will command the English Mastiff. This is an obligation that you have towards the English Mastiff as his owner. If you cannot take this charge, you must reconsider bringing him home. The most important thing that you need to do as the owner is channel his energies in the right direction. If your dog is given ample exercise, he will not indulge in practices like chasing too often.

5. Endearing Habits

There are some things about your English Mastiff that will just make you grow fond of him with each passing day. Chewing is one such habit that is common with the Mastiffs. This might be a matter of concern to most people who are worried about the belongings that the English Mastiff might happily chew into bits. Of course, you need not worry about this as the English Mastiff can be trained to chew only toys and large bones to fulfill his need to chew things.

Another habit of the English Mastiff that you cannot ignore is drooling. Now, drooling is more of a natural process than a real 'habit' in case of an English Mastiff. These dogs have a very loose and thick muzzle that falls over the upper lip. So, when the dogs eat or drink, they tend to drool a lot. Another thing that comes into mind is the size of the animal. Most people believe that drooling is a cooling mechanism of sorts as far as the English Mastiff goes. Remember that a dog as large as the English Mastiff requires a lot of food. So, if you are going to have an English Mastiff at home, be prepared for a lot of drooling. The drool is thick and has almost the same consistency as egg whites. If the English Mastiff is drooling at all times, even when there is no food or water involved, you must raise your concerns. This means that the English Mastiff is either stressed, scared or even unable to handle high temperature. You must, then, take adequate measures to make your English Mastiff feel comfortable and safe.

The last habit that I would like to mention is snoring. This is a habit that is not exclusive to an English Mastiff. All Mastiffs indicate that they are sound- asleep by snoring loudly. Even if your English Mastiff is sound asleep on the first floor, you will be able to hear his loud snores in the ground floor. Now, if you are a light sleeper, you might want to buy yourself a pair of ear plugs.

6. Versatility

A dog like the English Mastiff is an excellent choice because of its versatility of function. This breed makes for a great companion and also ensures that your home is well guarded and taken care of. The temperament of this dog is ideal as it helps you find a great companion in him. There is a dilemma that the English Mastiff is often confronted with. To begin with, he is a compulsive work dog. He takes his role as the guardian of the house extremely seriously. This is instinctive and you cannot remove this trait from the dog.

The English Mastiff will fulfill his duties as a guard dog while being a great companion. The appearance of the dog itself makes him very formidable. He has the head of a gargoyle and the body of a looming beast. With just these qualities he is able to keep intruders at bay. Now, for those who take a look at the English Mastiff, he seems like a lazy dog who is just lounging around. But, what most people don't know is that an English Mastiff is never in a state of inertia. He could just be resting or even sleeping but he will act instantly when he expects some danger to his property of family.

The English Mastiff always tries to save all his energy for when he actually requires it. So you will see him resting and lounging always. He is even tempered and is very calm at most times. The important thing to know about an English Mastiff is that he will wait, watch and then attack if necessary. These dogs are not like the German Shepherds or the other breeds that like to patrol. They will have a watchful eye on their home and property while they cuddle up on the couch or just wait by your feet.

7. Obedience and Agility

It seems almost unfair to expect agility of an English Mastiff. He is such a huge dog that his weight keeps him from being jumpy and active like the other breeds. While he does like to chase after a cyclist or a rabbit once in a while, do not expect your English Mastiff to appreciate it when you force him into going on a jog with or just run alongside a bicycle.

These dogs do not have too much stamina and will begin to drool when they are physically strained too much. Your English Mastiff will love the outdoors and will also play fetch, but at his own pace. Never try to rush the English Mastiff on the pretext of getting him good exercise, fresh air etc. One thing that the English Mastiffs love to do is swim. They enjoy their time in the water and will appreciate it if you take him swimming as often as you can. The water will also give him a break from the large weight that he needs to carry around all day. When you force an English Mastiff to exercise or do more that what his body is capable of, you can put him at the risk of overheating. This may result in cardiac issues or other conditions that might be fatal.

Remember, if you have an English Mastiff puppy at home, you must never over exercise him. This reduces the development of their limbs and also puts their skeletal structure at the risk of permanent damage. If you have an English Mastiff puppy, you must only take him for short walks. However, the usage of stairs should be limited. The reason you need to be so careful with the Mastiff is that they have a very high tolerance for pain. Due to this, their injuries often go unnoticed. You will see obvious signs and symptoms only when the condition is extreme.

Obedience is another thing that you can expect from the English Mastiff. However, you cannot expect him to obey your command as quickly as breeds like the Aussies and the Shepherds. Whenever you give your English Mastiff any command, he will wait, think about it and then react. Sometimes, it seems as if he is questioning your command itself. This was a big issue with people who wanted to include their English Mastiffs in shows. The Obedience judges often marked them very low as they seemed to not understand the commands at all. However, with increased knowledge about the breed and its behavior, this perception is soon changing and English Mastiff is receiving better marks for his obedience skills.

The English Mastiff is a spectacular breed. He is a majestic animal who is very aware that his master is in command. This makes you a lot more responsible for your English Mastiff. Most people treat their English Mastiff as a working dog and leave him on a large farm with tons of food and water. This is just wrong as these breeds required a lot of emotional reassurance. Sure, they are powerful and meant for hunts and fights but they tend to get very lonely and confused when they do not have a master.

Human company is very important for this breed as they have become accustomed to being around people and obeying them for centuries now. If you feel like you do not have it in you to spend time with the English Mastiff, you must never attempt to raise one. As most pet owners would agree, this is true for any pet.

If you are a first time pet owner, especially, the English Mastiff is not a good breed to bring home. You must have some experience with large dogs before you bring home an English Mastiff. You must have all the knowledge that you might need to take care of this breed and also keep him happy and content.

Chapter 7: Personality Rating for an English Mastiff

To make it easier for you to judge if the English Mastiff is the right breed for you, here is a quick rating of the breed. I have marked the most important qualities out of 5 to make sure that you understand how compatible you and the English Mastiff will be.

- Affection towards Owner- 5/5

- Aggression - 4/5

- Obedience - 4/5

- Functionality - 5/5

- Adaptability - 5/5

- Playfulness - 5/5

- Compatibility with dogs - 2/5

- Compatibility with children - 3/5

- Compatibility with smaller animals -3/5

- Intelligence - 5/5

- Activity level - 4/5

Chapter 8: Extending Your Home for an English Mastiff

When you are bringing an English Mastiff home, there are many things that you must do to make the house comfortable for him. Your preparations for bringing your English Mastiff home begin from the stage when you collect as much information as you might require about this breed. It is a great idea for you to share this information with other residents of your home before you decide to extend your home to a puppy.

1. Ask Yourself if You are Prepared?

Although the English Mastiff seems like an excellent breed to bring home, you will have to really reason with yourself whether you are a suitable owner or not. Many dog owners get carried away by the appearance and majesty of the breed without considering many important factors when they bring home an English Mastiff puppy. Here are a few questions that you should ask yourself when you decide to bring home an English Mastiff:

- Do you have the time to make a commitment and being a full time owner to the English Mastiff?
- Is your home large enough to house an English Mastiff?
- Does your English Mastiff have enough place outside to go on a walk or just lounge around?
- Are there any members in your family, pets and children, who might be put at risk if you bring home an English Mastiff?
- Will you be able to afford the care required for an English Mastiff?

49

You see, whenever we decide to bring home a pet, we always believe that we will be able to "walk them everyday", "wash them every week" etc. These commitments cannot be frivolous as a pure breed like an English Mastiff requires you to be hands on master. Consider your life on a long-term basis when you decide to make that commitment. What if you have to move? What if your schedules change? Are you likely to make drastic changes in your life that might affect the dog? Never make a momentary decision as you are jeopardizing the well being of a beautiful creature.

2. Making a Commitment

Once you decide to bring an English Mastiff home, it is a given that you understand your responsibilities towards that dog. It means that you have chosen an English Mastiff after carefully studying the behavior and the needs of the breed. This is the breed that fits best into your lifestyle and your requirement, and you are, therefore, making this choice.

When you begin to look for a breeder and actually have found one, you are closer towards making your commitment to the breed. You have voluntarily looked for an individual who is responsible towards this breed at a very professional level. If you find a good breeder, you have found someone to help you and your puppy settle down with each other and lead a life together.

I recommend that before you make that commitment, you spend some time with at least one puppy pack. This gives you a chance to study the behavior and personality of each puppy, thereby finding a particular one that best suits your needs. There are several things that you can look for when you are observing a pack of puppies. Some puppies will be evidently outgoing, others will be very quiet and observant. Some of them will display leadership skills that will take you by surprise. So, you can make a wise decision based on what characteristics you require with your puppy. Once you know that a puppy is appealing to you, do not think twice. He is the one you want to bring home.

This time that you spend with a puppy pack does one more thing for you. You will be able to understand the dynamics of an English Mastiff and also realize that it is, in fact, not the right breed for you. It is best to come to this realization before you bring an English Mastiff home.

If you have friends who have an English Mastiff at home, you might also want to spend some time with the adult dogs to understand how easy or complex it is to have an English Mastiff at home. Once you are sure, you can make that leap of commitment and bring home your very own bouncy little English Mastiff!

3. Preparing your Home

Imagine if you were bringing home a newborn baby. There would be several things that you would take care of before the baby arrives. You will need toys; a crib and other supplies that will help you take care of your baby. An English Mastiff puppy too is just like a baby that is covered in loose and wrinkled fur! So there is a lot of preparation required in your home and for your family to bring home a special breed like the English Mastiff.

The one thing that you must remember is that the English Mastiff puppy is coming in to a space that is going to become his home as well. So, the types of preparations that you will make depend entirely on what you expect of the dog. At all times, you are in charge, so you will not bring a puppy into your home and simply let him take over. For instance, if you are bringing home an English Mastiff to be a strict working dog, the bedding and the space that he will use will be entirely different from an English Mastiff who is brought home for companionship.

While you are limiting the space that the English Mastiff can use and the freedom that he will have in your home, be careful to ensure that he does not feel claustrophobic in your home. Space and warmth are the two most essential things that you must ensure for your English Mastiff. Of course, I am not talking about warmth in terms of temperature! Your puppy is going through a major transition because he is leaving a home that he is already used to, to make another space his home. He is taken away from the warmth and comfort of his mother and his littermates to live among completely new beings.

So, as the owner, it is your responsibility to make sure that you do not deprive the dog of anything. There are many supplies that are mandatory when you bring home an English Mastiff. You must also try your best to ensure that he does not feel traumatized. One good idea is to ask your breeder to give you a toy that the puppy is fond of. There must be some form of familiarity that will help your puppy get accustomed to a new place.

Treat the English Mastiff like a baby and avoid everything that you would avoid with a child. That is when you will gain the confidence and love of your English Mastiff. The good news is that most of the English Mastiff puppies are well mannered and even tempered by nature which makes it a lot easier on the owners to make this new member in the family feel welcomed and extremely comfortable.

4. Introducing your Puppy to your Family

The idea of bringing a puppy home is very exciting for anyone! The members in your family, especially the kids, will want to pet the dog, play with him and even cuddle. This can be uncomfortable for the puppy as the sights, sounds and sensations of your home are completely new to him. Here are some ground rules that you must establish when you are bringing an English Mastiff home to your family:

• The introduction should be low key. Remember that your puppy is extremely anxious as he has been brought away from his mother and the breeder who are familiar to him. If you smother him with affection, you will actually drive him away from you and frighten him.

• Human contact is necessary but must be controlled and gentle in the beginning. The puppy will while and cry a lot. So you must be able to console him. Just let him be and speak to him in a soft voice.

• Do not turn the music or television on too loudly when the puppy is new to your home. This will frighten him out f his wits and make the whole experience of coming into your home traumatic.

• There will be no guests or friends visiting him till he is entirely comfortable. Of course, socializing is necessary for the English Mastiff, but you must try you best to not overwhelm him.

• Allow him to explore the place without any disturbance. Unlike pets like cats, your English Mastiff does not require any confinement or separate room to get used to the new environment. All he needs to do is sniff around and get used to the common sights and sounds in your home.

5. Puppy Proofing your Home

Yes, there is such a thing as puppy proofing your place. While you are busy making your home comfortable for your English Mastiff, you may forget to make the home secure for him. There are several areas in your home that might be dangerous for you puppy. You may also have some regular habits like spraying cockroach spray or using rodent kill to keep your home free from pets. These are things you must reconsider before you bring home a puppy.

The first thing to do before you bring home a puppy is to ensure that you take necessary precautions that will prevent the puppy from getting into things that you do not want him to get into. If you know that there are objects that might threaten the safety of your puppy, keep them closed or make all the arrangements to make sure puppy is unable to reach them.

Remember that a puppy will be inquisitive. He will investigate, sniff and even chew objects that seem new and interesting to him. So another reason for you to puppy proof your home is to ensure that none of your belongings are ruined in the process. For instance, if you have breakable objects that the puppy might knock over, you should make sure that they are away from the reach of the puppy. At the same time you must not restrict a full run of your little one.

There are some things that cannot be put away. For instance, consider the electrical cords. While they are potentially dangerous for the dog, you cannot do without them. In such cases, you might consider tying up the wires so that the puppy is unable to get it out and chew it. Of course, you cannot convince or 'train' your puppy to stay away from these cords. The best you can do is not allowing it to be dangling around and available easily to the English Mastiff.

Even when your puppy is kept in a crate, there is no guarantee that he is entirely safe. Make sure that there aren't any harmful objects like home cleaners or other chemicals around the crate of the puppy. If the puppy is able to reach out with his paw and grab the object or spill it over, you still are putting him in danger.

Drinking out of the toilet water bowl is something that every puppy loves to indulge in. It is your job to keep the lid closed at all times to prevent this. Drinking the water from a toilet bowl might cause harmful infections and severe damage to the puppy's health.

This covers just the inside of your home. You must also ensure that the area outside your home is safe for your puppy as you cannot restrict him to your home. When the puppy is too young, make it a point to not let the puppy into the outdoors without any supervision. He should be allowed to walk around the yard and explore while you are watching.

Just because your home is fenced, do not assume that your puppy is safe. The English Mastiff is a crafty and persistent creature. If he gets his mind on crossing the fence, he will make a rabbit hole or even jump across if you are not watching. The best thing to do is to make a fence that is really high and well inserted into the ground. For complete protection, the fence must be at least 8 feet high. You must also check that there are no gaps or holes in the fence. It is also important to keep the fence well maintained. Even a small notion that the fence can be crossed will make your puppy persistent to get across. Of course, considering the English Mastiff, your puppy may not be attempting to break out or get out of the house. All he is interested in doing is exploring the new space that he is in.

If you have a garden or a yard, you must make sure that there aren't any plants that have very thick and sharp thorns. When the puppy is young, his skin is delicate and he may have serious cuts and wounds if you do not tend and maintain your garden well.

6. Get Insurance

If you are bringing home a special pure breed like the English Mastiff, you must make sure that you get your pet completely insured. In some cases, pet insurance is mandatory to get your dog the license that is necessary to have him in the house legally.

Getting a pet insurance is equivalent to getting any sort of insurance, be it your own health insurance or car insurance. The idea is to get your dog's health insured so that he can get the right attention when necessary. There are several factors that determine the type of insurance policy that you will get. The premium that you pay on your insurance depends on three things:

• The age of your dog- the older your dog, the higher will the premium will be.

• The breed of your dog- the premium that you pay for dogs of a purer breed is higher as these dogs require expensive care and treatment.

• The type of coverage that you require- You must be sure of what you want your policy to cover. The coverage sum is also an important factor for your premium.

With most insurance policies, you should be able to get coverage for injuries due to accidents, common medical problems, poisoning and even severe terminal diseases like cancer. There are some policies that will also cover things like immunization, routine care, flea control prescription, annual checkups and also dental care. Of course these policies are quite expensive and require a higher premium payment.

When you consider the costs of going to the vet and getting your dog checked up thoroughly, you will realize that getting insurance is a great thing to do. In an untoward situation when your English Mastiff requires attention, you will be able to provide him with all the necessary care and attention without making any compromises.

Most pet owners neglect this rather important step towards pet care. In my personal experience, I have seen that the anxiety and the sorrow that the owners go through in case of medical emergencies is quite traumatic. So, I recommend that you speak to your breeder or even an insurance agent to get the right information about the policies that are available in the market. The best people to give you accurate advice are people who already have pet insurances for their little ones. They will be able to tell you why a certain policy will work and why another will fail.

To begin with, your pup might not be very affectionate and cuddly. Do not jump to conclusions that your pup has a behavior problem. It is just natural that your puppy will like to be by himself for a while. As he becomes more familiar around your home, each member of the family can take turns to get close to the pup. All you need to do is sit down and get to the level of your puppy. Then allow him to smell your hands, nibble at your fingers or just walk around your sniffing and contemplating. Doing this on a regular basis will make the English Mastiff more relaxed around you.

Dogs are some of the most compatible creatures when they are left with human beings. We all know that. Especially with a breed like the English Mastiff who is a full on family dog, you never have to worry about problems in this process. He will eventually get used to your and be playful and happy.

Pet guardians commonly ask themselves, when considering medical insurance for their dog, whether they can afford not to have it. On the one hand, in light of all the new treatments and medications that are now available for our dogs, that usually come with a very high price tag, an increasing number of guardians have decided to add pet insurance to their list of monthly expenses.
On the other hand, some humans believe that placing money into a savings account, in case unforeseen medical treatments are required, makes more sense.

Pet insurance coverage can cost anywhere from $2,000 to $6,000 USD (£1201 to £3604) over an average lifespan of a dog, and unless your dog is involved in a serious accident, or contracts a life-threatening disease, you may never need to pay out that much for treatment.

Whether you decide to start a savings account for your dog so that you will always have funds available for unforeseen health issues, or you decide to buy a health insurance plan, most dog lovers will go to any lengths to save the life of their beloved companions. Having access to advanced technological tools and procedures means that our dogs are now being offered treatment options that were once only reserved for humans.

Now, some canine conditions that were once considered fatal, are being treated at considerable costs ranging anywhere between $1,000. and $5,000. (£597 and £2,986) and more. However, even in the face of rapidly increasing costs of caring for our dogs, owners purchasing pet insurance remain a small minority.

In an effort to increase the numbers of people buying pet insurance, insurers have teamed with the American Kennel Club and Petco Animal Supplies to offer the insurance, and more than 1,600 companies, such as Office Depot and Google, offer pet insurance coverage to their employees as an optional employee benefit. Even though you might believe that pet insurance will be your savior anytime your dog needs a trip to the vet's office, you really need to be careful when considering an insurance plan, because there are many policies that contain small print excluding certain ages, hereditary or chronic conditions.

Unfortunately, most people don't consider pet insurance when their pets are healthy because buying pet insurance means playing the odds, and unless your dog becomes seriously ill, you end up paying for something that may never happen.

However, just like automobile insurance, you can't buy it after you've had that accident. Therefore, since many of us, in today's uncertain economy, may be hard pressed to pay a high veterinarian bill, generally speaking, the alternative of paying monthly pet insurance premiums will provide peace of mind and improved veterinarian care for our best friends.

Shop around, because as with all insurance policies, pet insurance policies will vary greatly between companies and the only way to know for certain exactly what sort of coverage you are buying is to be holding a copy of that policy in your hand so that you can clearly read what will and what will not be covered. Don't forget to carefully read the fine print to avoid any nasty surprises, because the time to discover that a certain procedure will not be covered is not when you are in the middle of filing a claim.

Before Purchasing a Policy

There are several considerations to be aware of before choosing to purchase a pet insurance policy, including:

Is your dog required to undergo a physical exam?
Is there a waiting period before the policy becomes active?
What percentage of the bill does the insurance company pay — after the deductible?
Are payments limited or capped in any way?
Are there co-pays (cost to you up front)?
Does the plan cover pre-existing conditions?
Does the plan cover chronic or recurring medical problems?
Can you choose any vet or animal hospital to treat your pet?
Are prescription medications covered?
Are you covered when traveling with your pet?
Does the policy pay if your pet is being treated and then dies?

When you love your dog and worry that you may not have the funds to cover an emergency medical situation that could unexpectedly cost thousands, the right pet insurance policy will provide both peace of mind and better health care for your beloved fur friend.
Keep in mind that usually your monthly or yearly premium will increase when your dog gets older.

TIP: Get your pet insurance BEFORE your dog has been to the vet with a health issue. In my case, one of my dogs had something wrong with his eyes and I went to the vet. I took an insurance policy 3 months later and the insurance asked me to give them the pet records. This results is that I now have an insurance policy that EXCLUDES anything to do with my dog's eyes.

7. First night in your home

The first night that the English Mastiff spends in your home is the most crucial one. Since he has had a rather adventurous day, he might not be entirely comfortable yet. Think of the day from your English Mastiff's point of view. He has come to your home in a car, probably. You must have placed him in the lap of the passenger or in a crate. Usually, English Mastiffs love to ride in the car. But, the first ride to your place, away from his litter, might not be as pleasant as you expected to be. Besides crying and wailing, the puppy may also urinate or have loose bowels due to anxiety. Relax! He is a baby! And if you want to be his mom, you must get used to this!

He then goes to the vet, gets a thorough exchange. Here, he is amidst several other anxious animals that are dreading their encounter with the vet. Since the English Mastiff is sensitive to these vibes, he will be really afraid. If your vet deworms and vaccinates him, the poor little guy will be eager to just get back to the nice 'breeder man'!

Then he comes into your home. He is adorable and everyone wants to get a piece of the cute little guy. He will resist this in the beginning but will enjoy it very soon. He will lick the hands of all the members in the house and wag his tail till he realizes that he misses his mom. If he has to meet other pets, especially unhappy cats, he will be a little wary.

After this, he gets to explore the new space around him. Hey! He has a new bed, a new yard and other new areas that he has never seen. He also likes you more not since you have probably given him his first meal. He then wanders around, experiencing so many new things that you would expect him to be exhausted.

So, you think he is ready or bed. You leave him on that nice cushion you got for him and leave him alone. Now, this is probably his first night entirely by himself. He does not have his littermates around him to cuddle up to. He is scared and lonely and probably cold. So, he will try to grab your attention by whining uncontrollably. It is easy for us to give in and try to simply comfort the puppy or just keep him next to you to stop him from whining.

This is a wrong thing to do as you will be setting the wrong tone for the rest of the nights in your home. If you keep him with you that night, he will expect that to happen all the time. Also, on the first night, put your puppy to sleep at about the same time that you would normally go to bed, unless you want to be up with him till 2 am for the rest of the nights! It is possible to get carried away when it is the first night of your puppy in your home. However, just allow him to get used to the environment and then calm himself down.

If you let your puppy whine and cry for a while, he will eventually fall asleep. Although this is heart rending, be strong and just check on him a couple of times without him realizing that he has your attention. If you succeed in keeping your will strong on the first night, you will be able to help your puppy cope faster.

Of course, there are some things that you can do to help make the first night at your place easier on your English Mastiff. Most breeders recommend that you take a piece of the puppy's original bedding along and place it with his new stuff to make him feel like there is something familiar around him. If you live in a cold place, you could also put a hot water bag with warm water beneath his bedding. But be sure that he is not able to get his paws on it or else you will have a soaking and very stressed out English Mastiff!

8. Puppy Problems that You need to Address

There are some habits that you will notice with your English Mastiff when he is a puppy. Although in the early stages, you cannot consider these habits as problems, they might affect the behavior of your English Mastiff if you ignore them in those years. Just as you consider disciplining a child important, you must also consider disciplining your English Mastiff.

There are other reasons why, you as the owner of a Mastiff, have a greater responsibility in doing so. Remember that your English Mastiff is a very powerful dog. If you are unable to take proper care of him, you will make him a threat to your guests and even your own family. You must understand that it is a basic need to be able to control a large dog like the English Mastiff. For this, you must shower him with attention in the early years so that he understands who his master is!

Here are some common puppy problems that you must address in order to make sure that your English Mastiff grows up to be an elegant and handsome fellow.

Socialization

This is something that you must do right in the beginning. You cannot expect your English Mastiff to socialize as effectively even when he is 4 or 5 months old. The moment your puppy gets used to the ambience in your home, you must start the socialization of your English Mastiff puppy.

To begin with, Socialization is a fine chance to show your English Mastiff off to your friends. Now that you have decided to own such a magnificent creature, you must also enjoy some green eyed jealousy that you are bound to be on the receiving end of. After all, your friends are going to wish that the adorable fur ball was in their homes instead of yours! Well, this is just an excerpt from my own life, at the time when I unveiled my English Mastiff to my pals. I am sure this is an experience that you will also become familiar with soon!

Now, let's get down to some business and talk in detail about the socialization process itself. The socialization process of your English Mastiff begins with the breeder. Once you bring him home, it is your responsibility to continue this process and turn him into a dog who is comfortable in his surroundings. The first 3 months of socialization are the most critical ones.

Drawing parallels with children, again, you must understand that the mind of a English Mastiff pup is also a blank slate. The interactions and the experiences that he has in his earliest days help him form an impression of the outside world. It is this learning that will stick with him forever. You see, it is not enough if your puppy is accustomed to your home and family. He must meet other people and also experience new places in the initial stages. If this is not done correctly, there are two things that will happen- he will either become too shy and afraid or he will be excessively aggressive.

In the first three months, you must get as many people to meet him as possible. Avoid interactions with their pets during this time as he will still not be completely vaccinated. The next socialization phase that you must be very attentive is between 8 to 10 months of age. This phase is also known as the fear phase. During this time, every interaction that your English Mastiff has with the world must be positive and gentle. This is also the time when he is fully vaccinated and will be making his way into the real big bad world.

When you get a green signal from your vet to take the English Mastiff out and allow him to interact with other pets as well, you must spend as much time with him as you possibly can. Include him in all your activities, take him out to cafes that are pet friendly or even fix 'park times 'to make him familiar with new people and new experiences. Be very attentive when your pet is interacting with new people, especially children. Any bad experience will make him create a mental response mechanism that will stay with him forever.

Let's assume that your English Mastiff met an excited little child for the first time. The kid, in his excitement, ended up manhandling the puppy. Another possibility is that your English Mastiff was equally excited and nipped the child two hard. Both situations lead to negative responses. In the first case, your English Mastiff feels pain and in the second case, he probably got a sound scolding from you. The result is that your English Mastiff will now become afraid of children or will become aggressive towards them. Of course, in the earliest days of socialization, you can still reverse his impressions. However, if this happens in the fear phase, the reversal process can be a lot more challenging.

All the things that your English Mastiff learns in the formative years will greatly affect how your English Mastiff responds to situations in the future. The more he is petted and handled by people and is made to interact with other animals, the better it is for him. Just make sure that he is supervised at all stages and also that you protect him and reassure him in case negative experiences manage to slip in.

Nipping

When your puppy begins to teethe, he will feel like chewing on things to soothe his aching gums. The most common targets for your puppy's teething needs are your fingers. It is adorable when it begins but when the teeth of your puppy make their way through the gums, this nipping can be quite painful!

This behavior must not be curbed. It is a natural progression in your puppy's formative years. So, all you need to do is redirect his attention to other things. To get your puppy to stop chewing on your toes and fingers, the first step is to make it clear to him that it is not cute anymore! Say No in an affirmative voice when he begins to chew or nip at your toes. Sometimes, several No's might be in order to get your puppy to understand that you really mean business! The next step is to replace your finger with a chewing toy.

Using a toy is extremely important as your puppy needs to comfort himself with some chewing. However, if you fail to redirect his attention, he might even target your favorite shoe or furniture to fulfill his needs. You definitely do not want him to damage your stuff and others' stuff. So buy him loads of chewable toys.

The next step is to tell him what he can chew and what he must not chew. For this, you must respond with a firm no when he is chewing on something that is not meant for him!   On the other hand, when you see that he is chewing on the toy, praise him or even give him a treat as a reward. This training mechanism will go a long way in determining how your English Mastiff's chewing habits shape up.

When your English Mastiff grows up, you must try to get him out of the habit of chewing. You cannot entirely prevent an adult dog from chewing, but you can definitely ensure that he does not damage other things. The most common reason for adult- dog chewing is boredom. If your English Mastiff is simply lounging around or watching TV with you, he might want something to chew upon. A dog bone is the best thing you can get him to help him relive his boredom.

Nipping and chewing must be curbed for safety reasons as well. You, as the owner, might be familiar with your English Mastiff's nipping habits. For a child or a stranger this might be a scary thing and if they respond with a scream in fear, your English Mastiff might attack them for the sudden response. Also, the nipping of your English Mastiff gets more powerful as he grows up. He might never mean and harm but, he may also not be fully aware of the power of his bite.

Crying

Now, it is not possible for you to be with your English Mastiff at all given times. There may be instances when you will have to step out of your home or probably leave him on his own for a while. You may do this only when you thing that he is old enough to look after himself without getting too afraid.

If you are out of his range of vision, you can expect your English Mastiff to cry and whine. His goal is to grab your attention and make sure that you know that he is around. The last thing the English Mastiff wants is to be forgotten by his owner. The whining and crying will be a challenge for you to cope with in the beginning. When you hear your puppy whine, it will simply break your heart. But, it is also necessary for your English Mastiff to be able to spend time on his own. That way, when you really have to leave the house or probably go out for work, he will not feel so anxious.

Crying and whining is a response to anxiety that the English Mastiff feels in your absence. To make sure he does not hurt himself or get into trouble, you must leave him in the crate in the beginning. Training your English Mastiff to like the crate and be comfortable in it is also a part of the 'leaving alone' process. Unless he feels fully secure and safe inside the crate, he will not stop crying and whining incessantly.

The first step is to make the crate cozy. Add comfortable bedding that is warm and soft. Then, you can leave his favorite toy in the crate to keep him comforted in his perilous time alone. The next step is to make him associate positive experiences with the crate. There are several pet owners who will confine their pet to a crate when he does something naughty. This form of punishment will make him associate the crate with negative experiences. So, if you do this and leave the puppy in the crate, he is probably whining as he thinks that he is punished for doing something wrong.

Once the crate is ready, your challenge is to make him feel like it is okay to be on his own for a while. Start placing him in the crate for short periods of time to begin with. In the beginning, he must not be left alone for more than 30 minutes. After that, you may gradually increase the time frame when you see that he is comfortable for this initial duration. Toys will help keep him occupied so that he does not miss you too much.

It is also a good idea to keep him in the crate while you are still in the room for the first few days. That will prevent him from whining and he will also get comfortable in the room. Give him some toys to play with and slowly slip away from the room when he is unaware. If he has not been fussy and noisy while you were away, reward him with a treat.

When you think your puppy is ready to stay by himself for longer time periods, you can still do a few things to be sure that he does not get anxious. You can leave the radio on softly so that the voices of people will trick him into believing that he is not alone. Always leave your puppy in a crate when he is alone. Avoid leashes as they may harm themselves while trying to break free from the leash.

Tackling these puppy problems help in three ways:

• It will tell your puppy who the master is!
• It will make your puppy comfortable with new people and experiences.
• The chances of your puppy growing up to be aggressive or afraid are fewer.

The initial years require a lot of attention and understanding of your puppy's mentality. Unless, you are prepared for this, you might not want to bring a English Mastiff puppy home.

9. Getting an English Mastiff

If you are looking for a Mastiff puppy, there are several places where you can get one. First, you can check with your vet to see if there are any breeders who are specialized in Mastiffs. With a breed like the Mastiff, you must be assured of its purity. So, you must always look for a breeder who will issue a pedigree certificate for your puppy.

The second step is to check the Internet for puppy sales. If you find someone who you think is reliable, make sure you visit him and check out the breeding conditions before you actually invest in a Mastiff.

The last and most recommended step is to check with fellow Mastiff owners. They will be able to put you on to the person they got their puppy from. These people are the most reliable source as they have already been tried and tested.

When you are planning to purchase a Mastiff, make sure you make all the enquiries even if you are at the risk of sounding too pushy. This is an expensive breed to buy and an even more expensive breed to care for if there are unwarranted health issues.

Is it at all possible to adopt a dog as large and challenging as the English Mastiff? This is a question worth asking before you get your hands into something you simply cannot manage. You see, Mastiffs are usually single master dogs. So if you are bringing a English Mastiff home, you must understand that you are not the master that he is accustomed to. Also a large dog who is not trained to fit into your lifestyle can be dangerous for you and your family. However, if you must adopt a English Mastiff, there may be some valuable factors that you must consider.

To begin with, you must know where to adopt a English Mastiff from. The best place to find out is the Internet where you can get several genuine shelters and rescue centers where you can get your dog from. These websites also allow you to check specific things like house training and also put in special requests so that you can find a dog that will fit perfectly into your lifestyle. There are also regular "need a home" ads that appear in local newspapers. You can review these ads and make a choice. Today, you also have the option of the social media where you can post requests for adoption. There are also several pages on these sites that you can visit and check for English Mastiffs for adoption. You may even ask your friends and relatives to keep an eye out for these dogs.

You may also check with the experts in your vicinity. The decision to bring home a English Mastiff is not an easy one. You must speak to these experts and discuss with them to understand if this is the best choice of dog for you. The experts that you must include in your research are vets, groomers, breeds, walkers and even people who own these dogs. Once you are convinced with the recommendations that you get from your reliable network, you may go ahead and make a decision.

The best place to look for a English Mastiff is a breed club. Usually, most breed clubs have rescue groups that are focused on the rescue and treatment of a specific breed. In your case, you can look at English Mastiff Clubs. These groups will try to get you the perfect dog to take home to your family.

The problem with regular shelters is that they may hide certain facts pertaining to the dog that you are planning to adopt. You see, dogs that are put in rescue homes are abandoned, abused or injured. In all cases, the dog has suffered a terrible trauma and must be given special care and attention. If you are unsure of how to take care of the dog, you must definitely not bring him home. That way you are putting his and your life at risk. With breed rescue groups, you will receive all the details of the issues that the dog has. They will also give you tips to take care of the dog. If needed these breed rescue groups also double as foster homes for your beloved Mastiff.

You must be equipped with all the information about the breed. For this, you must know what to ask the breeder when you decide to adopt a English Mastiff. Some vital information for a dog that you want to adopt includes his age, his agility, his ability to mingle with other animals, his house training level, evident displays of aggression including biting and attacking someone and health issues that you must be aware of.

When you have the information that you need and you decide to adopt, you must get a valid contract with your breeder or the rescue group. This document lists certain responsibilities on both ends. Sometimes you may end up with a dog who is impossible to take care of. To avoid this, you can make use of the Internet to understand what conditions are ideal and appropriate for you as the future pet parent. Remember that you are also entitled to certain rights as the person adopting the puppy. There are also some recourses that you must be aware of.

Once you have adopted your English Mastiff, make sure you take him to a vet. Whether he is a puppy or an adult, he must be examined thoroughly by a vet to check for obvious health issues. Once your vet has spotted these problems, he will be able to give you the appropriate preventive healthcare plan to maintain the health of your Mastiff.

In my personal opinion, adopting a dog like the English Mastiff is best for people who have ample experience with a large dog. If you are a first time owner, you must consider a different breed altogether unless you have ample support and experts to help you.

10. Socializing

Introducing a dog to your family is a challenging experience when you are dealing with specific breeds who depict very unique behaviors. The biggest challenge for any pet owner is getting his new pet to interact and get accustomed to resident pets in your home. There are several things that you must keep in mind to make sure that this interaction is peaceful, without any fights and injuries. It requires a lot of effort from you end as animals tend to get extremely possessive of their owners and their family. Here are a few tips to help you ease your English Mastiff into your home.

This is something that you must do right in the beginning. You cannot expect your English Mastiff to socialize as effectively even when he is 4 or 5 months old. The moment your puppy gets used to the ambience in your home, you must start the socialization your English puppy.

To begin with, socialization is a fine chance to show your English Mastiff off to your friends. Now that you have decided to own such a magnificent creature, you must also enjoy some green eyed jealousy that you are bound to be on the receiving end of. After all, your friends are going to wish that the adorable fur ball was in their homes instead of yours! Well, this is just an excerpt from my own life, at the time when I unveiled my English Mastiff to my pals. I am sure this is an experience that you will also become familiar with soon!

Now, let's get down to some business and talk in detail about the socialization process itself. The socialization process of your English Mastiff begins with the breeder. Once you bring him home, it is your responsibility to continue this process and turn him into a dog who is comfortable in his surroundings. The first 3 months of socialization is the most critical one.

Drawing parallels with children, again, you must understand that the mind of a English Mastiff pup is also a blank slate. The interactions and the experiences that he has in his earliest days help him form an impression of the outside world. It is this learning that will stick with him forever. You see, it is not enough if your puppy is accustomed to your home and family. He must meet other people and also experience new places in the initial stages. If this is not done correctly, there are two things that will happen- he will either become too shy and afraid or he will be excessively aggressive.

In the first three months, you must get as many people to meet him as possible. Avoid interactions with their pets during this time as he will still not be completely vaccinated. The next socialization phase that you must be very attentive is between 8 to

10 months of age. This phase is also known as the fear phase. During this time, every interaction that your English Mastiff has with the world must be positive and gentle. This is also the time when he is fully vaccinated and will be making his way into the real big bad world.

When you get a green signal from your vet to take the English Mastiff out and allow him to interact with other pets as well, you must spend as much time with him as you possibly can. Include him in all your activities, take him out to cafes that are pet friendly or even fix 'park times 'to make him familiar with new people and new experiences. Be very attentive when your pet is interacting with new people, especially children. Any bad experience will make him create a mental response mechanism that will stay with him forever.

Let's assume that your English Mastiff met an excited little child for the first time. The kid, in his excitement, ended up manhandling the puppy. Another possibility is that your English Mastiff was equally excited and nipped the child two hard. Both situations lead to negative responses. In the first case, your English Mastiff feels pain and in the second case, he probably got a sound scolding from you. The result is that your English Mastiff will now become afraid of children or will become aggressive towards them. Of course, in the earliest days of socialization, you can still reverse his impressions. However, if this happens in the fear phase, the reversal process can be a lot more challenging.

All the things that your English Mastiff learns in the formative years will greatly affect how your English Mastiff responds to situations in the future. The more he is petted and handled by people and is made to interact with other animals, the better it is for him. Just make sure that he is supervised at all stages and also that you protect him and reassure him in case negative experiences manage to slip in.

a) Initial days

The first few days of your new dog's interactions with the resident pets is the most crucial period. There are several things that can go wrong if you allow any negative experiences to creep in when you are just bringing your English Mastiff home.

If the pet that you have is a large one, like another Mastiff or even another English Mastiff, you must make sure that he stays away from the new puppy. There must be no chance encounter that is unsupervised or unprotected. The best thing to do is to keep your puppy in a confined space until you have the time to make that interaction possible. You may even keep your puppy in a crate and leave him in a common area with the resident pet. Even when your English Mastiff is in the crate, he must be able to see you around that space. That will give him a feeling of security. However, if you simply leave him alone in the crate with the resident pet in the room, he might get terrified. This will make him associate the crate with negative experiences, making it very difficult for you to crate train him in the future.

Another simple thing to do is to separate the living areas for the two pets during this initial period. You may even have to move your resident pet's feeding area to a calmer and quieter one to help him escape the sudden introduction of the new puppy. If this is an approach that you opt for, make all the changes well in advance. The resident pet must never feel like you are trying to shun him away and make place for the new pet in your home.

On the other hand, if your resident pet is tiny and is usually in a crate, make sure you leave the crate in the same room as your English Mastiff at important times like the feeding hour or even during naptime. This will let the two animals get used to each other while maintaining a safe distance. Encourage your English Mastiff to spend as much time near the crate as possible. For this, you can use simple tricks like placing the food bowl or even a favorite toy of your English Mastiff close to the crate. While there is no real danger when such interactions are unsupervised, it is recommended that you stay close to comfort either animal if there is any negative reaction. You need not place the crate in the room always. This is an exercise that must be repeated on a regular basis.

Take your puppy everywhere with you and introduce them to many different people of all ages, sizes and ethnicities. This will be easy to do, because most people will automatically be drawn to you when they see you have a puppy because few humans can resist a cute puppy.

Most humans will want to interact with your puppy and if they ask to hold your puppy, this is a good opportunity to socialize your puppy and show them that humans are friendly. Do not let others (especially young children) play roughly with your puppy or squeal at them in a high-pitched voices because this can be very frightening for a young puppy. As well, you do not want to teach your puppy that humans are a source of crazy, excited energy. Be especially careful when introducing your puppy to young children who may accidentally hurt your puppy, because you don't want your dog to become fearful of children as this could lead to aggression issues later on in life. Explain to children that your puppy is very young and that they must be calm and gentle when playing or interacting in any way.

b) Special priority to the resident pet

If there is one thing that pets hate, it is sharing their territory and their master's attention. Usually, most of the negative reaction from the resident pets towards the new puppy is because the new member of the family gets all the attention. It is quite natural as everyone in the house wants to pet the new puppy. They all fuss over him and want to play with him, feed him and simply be around him. No resident pet will appreciate this.

You must understand that this is a very difficult time for the existing pet. So, as the owner, it is your job to make him feel just as special as ever. You may even have to try additional methods to make him the centre of your attention to avoid the development of feelings like anger and jealousy towards the new pet. Here are some simple things that you can do to make this phase comforting for your resident pet.

• Always show your resident pet that he is priority when it comes to feeding. So, if you have scheduled three meals for your new puppy, divide the meal for your resident dog into three portions as well. Try to feed them in the same room. During this time, feed the resident dog first and then provide your new puppy with his meal.

• When it comes to playtime, your resident pet gets to do what he loves most. When you come home after work, greet your resident pet first and then attend to the new pet. The idea is to tell you resident pet that he is just as important as he always was.

• Your new puppy must never be given the chance to push the resident pets aside to get your attention. If you are playing with your new puppy and the resident pet comes to you, attend to him immediately. Talk to him, play with him and pet him immediately. Do not wait until you are done playing with your puppy to attend to your resident pet.

• Dominance is a big issue with resident pets, especially dogs. This is also the reason for most of their fights with the new addition in your family. So there are simple gestures that you can follow to make your resident pet feel like he is still the 'senior' pet in the family. A simple example of this is, when you are taking the stairs, make sure your resident pet is allowed to go up first, followed by the new pet.

Although these things seem very trivial and meaningless, to an extent. They mean a lot to your resident pets. If you can follow these tips diligently, you can be sure that your home will be free from fights, jealousy and most importantly, cuts and bruises!

c) If your resident pet is a dog
When you introduce a dog to another dog, the dynamics of that meeting is very different. It is far from what you will experience with smaller pets like cats. There are some precautionary

measures that you must take when you are introducing your English Mastiff to a dog:

• Find a time when your resident pet is most calm. This is the time when you can arrange the introductory meeting. The nest time is when you have just fed your dog and he is ready for his afternoon lounging!

• Always be in control during these meetings. If your English Mastiff is still very young, you must make sure that both the dogs are on a leash. Ask your friend or a member of your family to help you out. Let the other person hold on to the English Mastiff on a leash. Then put your resident dog on a loose leash and cautiously approach your new puppy.

• This is a trying time for your dog. So give him many treats for being calm and comfortable around your new puppy. You must focus all your attention on your resident dog as he is most likely to strike or snap at the new puppy.

• If your dog is friendly and not resentful of the new puppy, you may take them both into your home. This indicates that your resident dog doesn't feel particularly threatened by the new puppy. However, this is also no reason to be negligent. You must still be as vigilant as you were in the initial days until they are both completely used to one another.

• The next thing is to plan the environment inside your home. If you have even the smallest doubts about your dog's reaction when the puppy is brought indoors, make all the necessary arrangements. You can place your puppy inside a play pet or a crate while you continue the interactions between the two pets.

• When two dogs are interacting, never interfere. There is always one of them who is more dominant than the other. While you would mostly expect your resident dog to react violently or negatively, sometimes the reaction of your puppy might surprise you. Irrespective of which one tries to be intimidating, you must never interfere unless you see potential danger to either one of them. In case of any spurt or outburst, take the side of your resident dog. Remember, you are making a change in his territory. So, it is only natural for him to have that rather dramatic reaction that is solely meant to put the new entrant in his place!

- In case the puppy you are introducing to your new dog is older, you must make sure that they are introduced on a long line. They must be allowed to greet each other while you simply preside or watch over the meeting. The resident dog is the one who gets to lead the new entrant in the family to your house. That gives him a place of authority where he can say, " Welcome to MY home"

Interactions between dogs when thoroughly supervised are usually very easy and simple. However, if your resident dog is very dominating by nature, you may want to put a muzzle on him. If you are uncertain of how to control these meetings, there are several professionals who can help you out.

d) What to watch out for
There are some signs that you must watch out for when you are introducing your English Mastiff to a resident dog:

- If your dog wags his tail, it doesn't necessarily mean that he is happy to have the new English Mastiff puppy in the house. You must look for other behavior patterns like slight growling, staring and lip curling that are signs of warning. Another important thing to watch out for is the stiffening of the body which indicates that your dog is not sure of how he must react to the puppy.
- A " play bow" is a common reaction among dogs. This is when the dog keeps his tail high while lowering his forelimbs to the ground. This is a sign that he wants to play and get to know the new dog. This, however, does not mean that the other dog is ready to play too. When you see one dog offer the play bow, you must also look at the reactions of the other dog. If he is not ready, you must not force them to play.

- Indifference is a great behavior for a first time meeting. Either one or both the dogs might be completely indifferent to the interaction. Even this behavior deserves a good deal of praising. You may give your dogs treats, too.

- The most normal behavior pattern is sniffing. If the body of your dogs is relaxed, you have little reason to worry. Encourage them to sniff each other as it is their way of getting acclimatized to the presence of the other.

- Look for any tension building between the two animals. If you notice even a little tension, call the meeting off. You can reintroduce them on another day or when they have completely calmed down. You can even start by keeping them apart and then reducing the distance as your shower them with praise and of course, treats.

e) If your resident pet is a cat

A cat would be pleased if you just get rid of the new puppy! They see the puppy as this looming creature that is put to get them. Instinctively, cats are intimidated by dogs. If your cat is confident, you have a whole different problem on your hands. A confident cat will allow the puppy to approach him without any hassles. However, he will also be quick to strike your English Mastiff on his nose when he feels too threatened. The whole deal here is up to you. Any reaction from your end that is too overwhelming will put your pets on edge. When you are introducing your English Mastiff puppy to a cat, here are some pointers that will be of great help.

- The puppy must be kept in an enclosed area with his favorite toy as a distraction. The cat must then be allowed to wander around in the room. One thing to know about cats is that they are very particular about their "free will". If you interfere with their 'free will' you will definitely put the cat off and will ruin the interaction. The only time you will interfere is when the puppy reacts violently to the presence of the cat.

- If the interaction between the two is calm, you can bring the puppy out of the cage and simply place him on a leash while the two animals share their space.

With cats and dogs, there is a chance that they will not be able to get along immediately.
If that happens, all you need to do is keep them in separate enclosures till your English Mastiff has been trained to understand the concept of " No" and until you are able to control him with a leash.

f) Within Different Environments
It can be a big mistake not to take the time to introduce your puppy to a wide variety of different environments because when they are not comfortable with different sights and sounds, this could cause them possible trauma later in their adult life.

Be creative and take your puppy everywhere you can imagine when they are young so that no matter where they travel, whether strolling a noisy city sidewalk or along quiet seashore, they will be equally comfortable.

Don't make the mistake of only taking your puppy into areas where you live and will always travel because they need to also be comfortable visiting areas you might not often visit, such as noisy construction sites, airports or a shopping area across town.

Your puppy needs to see all sorts of sights, sounds and situations so that they will not become fearful should they need to travel with you to any of these areas.

Your puppy will take their cues from you, which means that when you are calm and in control of every situation, they will learn to be the same because they will trust your lead.
For instance, take your puppy to the airport where they can watch people and hear planes landing and taking off.

Take them to a local park where they can see a baseball game, or take them to the local zoo or farm and let them get a close up look at horses, pigs and ducks.

g) Loud Noises

Many dogs can show extreme fear of loud noises, such as fireworks or thunderstorms.

If you take the time to desensitize your dog to these types of noises when they are very young, it will be much easier on them during stormy weather or holidays such as Halloween or New Year's when fireworks are often a part of the festivities.

You can purchase CD's that are a collection of unusual sounds, such as vacuums or hoovers, airplanes, people clapping hands, and more, that you can play while working in your kitchen or relaxing in your living room or lounge.

When you play these sounds and pretend that everything is normal, the next time your puppy or dog hears these types of sounds elsewhere, they will not become upset or agitated because they have learned to ignore them.

Also make sure that you get your young puppy used to the sounds of thunder and fireworks at an early age because these types of shrieking, crashing, banging and popping sounds of fireworks or thunder can be so traumatic and unsettling for many dogs, that sometimes, no matter how much you try to calm your dog, or pretend that everything is fine, there is little you can do.

Some dogs literally lose their minds when they hear the loud popping or screeching noises of fireworks and start running or trying to hide and you cannot communicate with them at all.
Make sure that your dog cannot harm itself trying to escape from these types of noises, and if possible, calmly hold them until they begin to relax.

If your dog loses its mind when it hears these types of noises, simply avoid taking them anywhere near fireworks and if at times when they might hear these noises going off outside, play your inside music or TV louder than you might normally, to help disguise the exterior noise of fireworks or thunder.

As well, some dogs will respond well to wearing a *"ThunderShirt"* which is specifically designed to alleviate anxiety or trauma associated with loud rumbling, popping or banging noises. www.thundershirt.com

The idea behind the design of the ThunderShirt is that the gentle pressure it creates is similar to a hug that, for some dogs, has a calming effect.

Do not underestimate the importance of taking the time to continually (not just when they are puppies) socialize and desensitize your puppy to all manner of sights, sounds individuals and locations because to do so will be teaching them to be a calm and well balanced member of your family that will quietly follow you in every situation.

Pet guardians commonly ask themselves, when considering medical insurance for their dog, whether they can afford not to have it. On the one hand, in light of all the new treatments and medications that are now available for our dogs, that usually come with a very high price tag, an increasing number of guardians have decided to add pet insurance to their list of monthly expenses.

On the other hand, some humans believe that placing money into a savings account, in case unforeseen medical treatments are required, makes more sense.

Pet insurance coverage can cost anywhere from $2,000 to $6,000 USD (£1201 to £3604) over an average lifespan of a dog, and unless your dog is involved in a serious accident, or contracts a life-threatening disease, you may never need to pay out that much for treatment.

Whether you decide to start a savings account for your dog so that you will always have funds available for unforeseen health issues, or you decide to buy a health insurance plan, most dog lovers will go to any lengths to save the life of their beloved companions. Having access to advanced technological tools and procedures means that our dogs are now being offered treatment options that were once only reserved for humans.

Now, some canine conditions that were once considered fatal, are being treated at considerable costs ranging anywhere between $1,000. and $5,000. (£597 and £2,986) and more. However, even in the face of rapidly increasing costs of caring for our dogs, owners purchasing pet insurance remain a small minority.

In an effort to increase the numbers of people buying pet insurance, insurers have teamed with the American Kennel Club and Petco Animal Supplies to offer the insurance, and more than 1,600 companies, such as Office Depot and Google, offer pet insurance coverage to their employees as an optional employee benefit. Even though you might believe that pet insurance will be your savior anytime your dog needs a trip to the vet's office, you really need to be careful when considering an insurance plan, because there are many policies that contain small print excluding certain ages, hereditary or chronic conditions.

Unfortunately, most people don't consider pet insurance when their pets are healthy because buying pet insurance means playing the odds, and unless your dog becomes seriously ill, you end up paying for something that may never happen.

However, just like automobile insurance, you can't buy it after you've had that accident. Therefore, since many of us, in today's uncertain economy, may be hard pressed to pay a high veterinarian bill, generally speaking, the alternative of paying monthly pet insurance premiums will provide peace of mind and improved veterinarian care for our best friends.

Shop around, because as with all insurance policies, pet insurance policies will vary greatly between companies and the only way to know for certain exactly what sort of coverage you are buying is to be holding a copy of that policy in your hand so that you can clearly read what <u>will</u> and what will <u>not</u> be covered. Don't forget to carefully read the fine print to avoid any nasty surprises, because the time to discover that a certain procedure will not be covered is not when you are in the middle of filing a claim.

Before Purchasing a Policy

There are several considerations to be aware of before choosing to purchase a pet insurance policy, including:

Is your dog required to undergo a physical exam?
Is there a waiting period before the policy becomes active?
What percentage of the bill does the insurance company pay — after the deductible?
Are payments limited or capped in any way?
Are there co-pays (cost to you up front)?
Does the plan cover pre-existing conditions?
Does the plan cover chronic or recurring medical problems?
Can you choose any vet or animal hospital to treat your pet?
Are prescription medications covered?
Are you covered when traveling with your pet?
Does the policy pay if your pet is being treated and then dies?
When you love your dog and worry that you may not have the funds to cover an emergency medical situation that could unexpectedly cost thousands, the right pet insurance policy will provide both peace of mind and better health care for your beloved fur friend.
Keep in mind that usually your monthly or yearly premium will increase when your dog gets older.

TIP: Get your pet insurance BEFORE your dog has been to the vet with a health issue. In my case, one of my dogs had something wrong with his eyes and I went to the vet. I took an insurance policy 3 months later and the insurance asked me to give them the pet records. This results is that I now have an insurance policy that EXCLUDES anything to do with my dog's eyes.

Chapter 9: Supplies You Need for Your English Mastiff

Once you have a puppy at home, there are several things that you will need to keep handy in order to help your puppy get acclimatized to your home and to his new life easily. Some of these supplies are basic necessities when you bring just about any breed of dog home. Here is a quick checklist with tips on how to use them and make them useful for your English Mastiff.

1. Crate

You will come across many pet owners and breeders who will shun the use of crates as an act of cruelty. Of course, keeping a dog in a crate all the time is not the right approach. However, the crate itself can be of great help, especially if you are interested in presenting your English Mastiff at shows and events. So, if you come across people who look at you with disapproval at the pet store when you are purchasing a crate, you can probably tell them these simple things that make a crate a life savior.

Uses of the crate

The puppy crate serves several purposes. Some of them are:

- You can use a crate when you are taking your pet to the vet. Not everybody has another person to accompany them and their pet during their visit to the pet.

- It is a great tool to train your puppy to spend time on his own without feeling afraid or left out.

85

- You can use your crate to confine your pet in case of injuries. Sometimes, these injuries require your pet to be still or even keep away from people, other animals and even dirt to prevent infections. In such cases, you will find the crate rather useful.

- Often in pet shows, you find yourself waiting for your turn. The best way to keep your pet away from the anxiety backstage is to keep them in a crate with lots of water.

- Crates are very handy when you are travelling with your pet. Whether you are taking your pet in your car or transporting him via airplanes, you will find that crates are very useful.

- Some dogs enjoy sleeping in their crate. If the crate is lined with warm bedding and left open, your English Mastiff can go and rest in it whenever he wishes to.

Types of crates

There are basically two types of crates that are available:
- The Fiberglass type
- The Wired Type

The fiberglass type of crate is open in the front and contains wiring. The body of the crate is made from fiberglass. The wired type consists of mesh all around the body of the crate. The type of crate that you invest in depends entirely on the purpose of the crate. There are no real rules for this. Both types of crates offer their own advantages and disadvantages. A wired crate, for instance, is a lot more airy. It lets your dog be aware of what is going on around him. The fiberglass crate on the other hand, is extremely sturdy.

You must, of course, make sure the size is appropriate. A fully grown English Mastiff will need a super sized crate. Your dog must not feel too confined or uncomfortable in the crate in order to be able to spend ample time in the crate. What I recommend is that you invest in an adult dog sized crate in the very beginning. It is not feasible to buy them again and again as your English Mastiff is bound to grow faster than you expect. Also, crates are expensive and it would be impossible to keep purchasing new ones as your pet continues to grow.

2. Bedding

The bedding that you provide will determine how comfortable and relaxed your puppy will feel in your home. Before I go into the importance of the bedding you provide, let me talk to you a little about the ancestry of your English Mastiff. Like all dogs, your English Mastiff's ancestors, too, loved to make their own cozy dens. In these dens, the dogs used dried leaves as their preferred bedding material. In the modern times, you cannot really expect to have dried leaves strewn around your home. However, while you think that your English Mastiff is far removed from his doggie ancestors, there are some instincts that he holds on to till date. One such instinct is the need to sleep on a warm bed. So, as the owner, it is your job to keep your dog warm and safe:

Why is bedding important?

This might seem like a redundant question as the bedding is obviously meant for your English Mastiff to sleep in. However, the bedding is more important than your think. It is the key to getting your English Mastiff acclimatized to your home: Some important functions of the bedding are:

• It gives your English Mastiff a warm and comfortable place to sleep in when he is new in your home. Good bedding will reassure him that he is in a safe place.

• Having good bedding will allow your English Mastiff to heal faster in case he is injured or unwell. Items like the bedding will help him be at ease and hence heal faster.

• Your English Mastiff will be emotionally more secure when he has a warm bed to turn to incase he is upset by some event.

• Your English Mastiff will be well rested if he has good and clean bedding. Therefore, he will be more energetic and playful.

Choosing the right bedding

Of course, you cannot bring home a bag of dried leaves and keep replacing it! The most suitable bedding for your English Mastiff is the crate plate covered with a warm blanket. Here are some tips that will create the perfect bedding for your English Mastiff:

• The first bedding that you make must consist of a piece of the bedding that he was used to while he was with the breeder. If you can accomplish that, his anxiety will be reduced.

• Use a fabric that is thick enough to produce ample cushioning so that the dog does not feel the crate plate pressing into his bones.

• The fabric must be still. It should not be too smooth and flowy like satin or silk as it is very uncomfortable to sleep on. Picture yourself on a large bed with slippery sheets! How uncomfortable!

• The fabric of the bedding must not be rough. Friction between the dog's skin and the fabric can cause irritation and rashes.

• Run your hand over the bedding once when you have laid it. It should be free from bumps and should be completely even for your English Mastiff to sleep peacefully.
Once you have taken care of all of the above, you can be sure that your English Mastiff has a good bed to rest on. Another responsibility that you have is maintaining the bedding. Especially when your English Mastiff is a puppy, he might soil his bedding occasionally. You must wash the bedding immediately and have it replaced. Leaving the bedding unclean will leave an unpleasant smell in your home. Additionally the

bacteria and the germs that thrive on the blanket might lead to unwanted infections. Also, ensure that your English Mastiff's bedding is in an area where it is free from moisture and dust. This will make the bedding much easier to maintain. It will also ensure that your precious pet is always relaxed.

3. Toys

For any dog to get ample exercise, toys are a must. Of course, walking the dog, taking him for a swim etc are great options. However, toys serve an entirely different purpose when it comes to keeping your dog well exercised and also entertained. No matter what breed of dog you bring home, toys are a must. Just like children, puppies develop several skills when they play with toys.

Uses of toys

Toys have more than one purpose in a dog's life. Here are some benefits of toys that you simply cannot deprive your dog or yourself of:

• Dogs are essential in the teething years of your English Mastiff. Instinctively, these dogs simply love to chew as well. So if you do not want your fingers, shoes or any other personal belonging to become the target of your English Mastiff's gnaws, make sure you get him toys.

• Toys help keep your pet mentally stimulated. There are some toys that make sounds that your English Mastiff will love. It will help keep him active and excited.

• Toys are great for your English Mastiff and you to bond with one another. Using these toys to play with your English Mastiff will keep you completely entertained as well.

• Toys also help your English Mastiff feel comforted and at ease when they are new to your home or when they are troubled by things like vaccinations and illnesses.

- They are very useful in helping you train your English Mastiff. They act as great tools to generate the desired response from your English Mastiff.

- English Mastiffs get really attached to toys. So these toys ease things like change of homes as dogs associate a sense of familiarity with their toys.

Precautions to take with toys

While toys are great for your English Mastiff, they might e hazardous to the health of your English Mastiff if proper care is not taken. Here are some simple tips that will help make the use of toys safer for your English Mastiffs.

- Avoid squeaky toys that have a little squeaker inside. For a dog as powerful as the English Mastiff, there are chances that your dog will just destroy the squeaky toy in minutes, thanks to his powerful jaws. This is true even for puppies. The squeaker that is present in the toy might choke your puppy if you are not attentive. The best use for a squeaky toy is as training equipment.

- You must never get your English Mastiff soft toys either. He will rip it apart in seconds and will probably choke on the stuffing present in the toy.
- Always choose toys that are of good quality. Low costing toys compromise on the quality and use toxic paints to make the toys. These paints might be hazardous for your English Mastiff.
- English Mastiffs love to chew. Sometimes, they will chew their toys to an extent when it begins to fall apart. If your English Mastiff's toy is in that condition, you must make sure you get rid of it. If you ignore it, there are chances that your English Mastiff will choke on the parts that are falling apart.

Choosing toys

There are so many toys that are available in the market that you will definitely get confused when you go out for the first time. Everything looks like great fun for you and your dog. However you must choose toys that will definitely grab the attention of your dog. There are two things you must keep in mind when you buy toys for your English Mastiff. The toys must be durable. Toys like the nylon bone are perfect for your English Mastiff. Second, this toy must have certain scents and sounds that your English Mastiff will enjoy.

4. The Collar

We all know why a collar is important for your English Mastiff. The collar is your point of control for a dog as large as the English Mastiff. This is where you fix the lead and guide your dog when you are taking him for a walk, hold him back from strangers or keep him tied when required. The collar is also used for the identification of your dog and usually has details like his name, his license and the address to his home.

There are three basic types of collars that you can use for your English Mastiff effectively. These collars have varied functions and are necessary for different stages of your puppy's growth. Of course, you need to make sure that you choose durable and good quality collars for your English Mastiff. He is a powerful dog and will require more than a piece of canvas or leather to hold him back as he grows up. So you must use the following types of collars as your English Mastiff grows up:

The buckle collar:

This type of collar is ideal for a puppy that is still in his growing years. As the name suggests, this collar comes with a buckle that makes it possible for you to adjust the tightness of the collar. For obvious reasons, this is an extremely important function as far as your English Mastiff puppy is concerned.

When you put the buckle collar on the neck of your English Mastiff puppy, you must check the tightness on a daily basis. It doesn't matter if you loosened it just today, it might get really tight overnight. So, you know what the consequences will be if you forget to loosen the collar on a regular basis.

You may continue to use this type of collar for everyday use. It is best that you pick up one that is made of nylon or leather as these materials are most durable. While you can use a buckle collar even on an adult English Mastiff, you must have other types of collar that will be able to hold back the power of your English Mastiff. You must use a collar that will allow you to control your English Mastiff completely in case he goes on a complete aggression spree on your guests, for instance. For this, there are more specialized collars like the ones mentioned below.

The choke collar

This is a type of collar that I am not entirely a fan of. However, it has proved to be extremely useful when it comes to training my dogs. This type of collar is made of steel links that have been attached to each other with a buckle in the end. You can easily slip this collar around the neck of your English Mastiff.

The main purpose of this collar is to help you train your dog. The idea is to create enough pressure around his neck to make him uncomfortable. Instinctively, when your English Mastiff feels too much pressure around the neck, he will stop pushing through and resisting your training efforts.

This type of collar can also be very dangerous for your English Mastiff. It is very easy even for a dog as large as an English Mastiff to choke on this type of collar. So, when your English Mastiff is out playing or just lounging, you must never have the choke collar on. There are many ignorant pet owners who consider the choke collar a style statement for the dog. Since it makes their English Mastiff look more "butch", they prefer to leave it on without paying too much heed to the safety of the poor animal.

Remember, a choke collar is a rather cruel thing to use. It is only good when your English Mastiff is under your watchful eye.

The haltercCollar

This is easily the safest and the most humane type of collar that is available. This collar goes over the shoulder blades of your dog rather than his neck. So, it makes it much easier to hold a huge dog like the English Mastiff back when you use this type of collar. Using a collar like the halter is best recommended for dogs that are either too difficult to hold back or too tiny to use a choke collar on.

When you have decided that type of collar that you want to use on your English Mastiff, you can even have it customized to look more glamorous on your English Mastiff. You get several colors that you can choose as per the color of the coat of your dog. You can also have the collar studded with stones and other embellishments if your English Mastiff is a girl. Engravings on the collars are also common these days. Today, the collar is more than just another 'supply' for your dog. It is an accessory that you must choose very carefully to glam up your little English Mastiff.

You must also use the collar from a young age to ensure that your English Mastiff is comfortable wearing the collar on a regular basis. While nylon collars are most reliable, you can choose other materials that you think are strong enough for your English Mastiff's pull of power.

5. The Lead

Once you have the collar in place, you will need a lead to make the collar functional. A lead is extremely important to keep your English Mastiff in control. The problem with the lead is that it is not good enough to get a lead that is able to hold the strength of your English Mastiff back. The lead should also be able to withstand the constant chewing of your English Mastiff, especially when he is a puppy. While it is your job to ensure that the chewing habit is redirected towards other toys, there is absolutely nothing that will guarantee that your English Mastiff will keep his teeth off the lead.

So, the best type of lead to use would be the one that is made of nylon. These leads serve both purposes and are also quite easy to get. These leads are also very light in weight and are extremely comfortable for daily use. If you are using a nylon lead, you can be assured that it is much easier to put on a puppy who is just being introduced to the concept of leashes. It is light and does not feel like a big addition to the English Mastiff's physical space.

When you are getting your English Mastiff ready for training, you can switch to a leather lead. This type of lead is great to hold the English Mastiff back. However, there is no need to keep the leather lead on at all times. However, it is definitely recommended that you keep a spare set leather set handy at all times. You never know when your formidable English Mastiff needs a bit of calming down.

6. Cleaning Material

Keeping your English Mastiff clean is another important part of your job as a pet parent. We will talk in detain about the actual grooming equipments to keep your English Mastiff clean. You will need several other things besides the sponges and brushes to keep your English Mastiff clean.

When your puppy is still young and his training stages, you can expect a lot of mess at home on a regular basis. This is especially true when your English Mastiff has not been toilet trained. You must keep several old rags and pieces of paper handy to keep your home clean. You will also need cleaning liquids and detergents to really clean up thoroughly. Whatever chemicals you choose for your cleaning kit, make sure that they are pet friendly and free from toxins.

7. Bowls for Food and Water

This is perhaps the first thing you will pick up when you bring a pet home. There are two bowls that you will need for your English Mastiff. You will require one bowl for food and one bowl for water. Also, having a single set is not good enough. You will need one set of bowls to keep inside your home and one set of bowls to place outside. It then depends on the English Mastiff where he chooses to eat!

You can choose between plastic bowls and stainless steel bowls. The ones made of steel are preferred as they are sterilized and safer to use. Another advantage is that your English Mastiff will not chew upon a steel bowl. However, he will completely ruin his bowl if it is made of plastic.

Since the English Mastiff is a large dog, you will also need a small stool or stand to place the bowls on. This will keep the food and water closer to the level of the dog and he won't have to stretch too much to eat and drink. This simple facility will also prevent digestive problems like bloating and gastric torsion. He will be able to digest his food easily and, thus, remain healthier.

There are several other supplies that you can include in your list depending upon your lifestyle and the ambience that your puppy will grow up in. You can include several grooming supplies, doggy t-shirts, accessories and even medicines in this list. It all depends completely on what you need the most for your English Mastiff to have a happy life. There are several pet stores that you can pick up these supplies from. These days with many more people interested in having pets at home, there might even be a separate aisle for these products in your local super market.

Chapter 10: Daily Care for an English Mastiff

You need to take care of several things on a daily basis to maintain the health and well being of your English Mastiff. Some of these daily care activities like feeding and exercising might seem like a walk in the park. However, when it comes to a dog like the English Mastiff which is a separate and special breed, you will have to take special care at various stages of his growth to ensure that he is getting everything that he requires to grow into a healthy dog.

1. Feeding your English Mastiff

Feeding an English Mastiff is very challenging. He is a big dog, so he requires a special diet that is nutritious and suitable for his metabolic needs. Of course, you cannot feed a puppy the same thing that you would feed an English Mastiff. I recommend that you read this chapter over a couple of times to understand how you must feed your English Mastiff. When you actually step out to pick up some food for your English Mastiff, it can be seriously intimidating as there are so many options available, each seemingly better than the other.

Of course, there are various brands of foods that are available. But, it you really look at it, there are three types of foods that are available for dogs: moist food, semi moist food and dry kibble. While most owners simply give their English Mastiff dry kibble as it is the most inexpensive option, it is not good enough to fulfill all the dietary requirements of your English Mastiff. A combination of dry kibble with moist food is, undoubtedly, the best thing for your English Mastiff. These moist foods consist of almost 70% of water and are great for your English Mastiff. On the other hand, you English Mastiff will absolutely love semi moist food because of the taste and texture. However, with the amount of sugar that these foods contain, I recommend that you never introduce your English Mastiff to this type of food at all!

As a rule, an English Mastiff must be fed at least 2 times a day as an adult and 3 times a day until he is six months old. You must never allow him to be free fed. Free feeding means simply leaving food in his bowl for him to eat when he wants. For an English Mastiff, there is no time when he does not feel like he needs food. Feed him on a timely basis for the best results. We will compare free feeding and scheduled feeding for you to understand better.

2. Free Feeding v/s Scheduled Feeding

There are several pet owners who are still debating on which feeding method is better for a dog. Honestly, this depends entirely upon the breed that you have at home. For this book, we will discuss about the types of feeding with the English Mastiff in mind.

What is the difference?

This is the basic need, to understand the difference between scheduled feeding and free feeding. Scheduled feeding is when your dog is given a fixed quantity of food at a fixed time. The number of times you feed the dog also depends upon the breed. Free feeding refers to simply leaving the food in the bowl for the dog to eat whenever he wishes to. Many owners opt for this feeding method as they feel satisfied that they are not missing meals because of the busy schedule.

What is best for my English Mastiff?

The concept of free feeding relies on the fact that a dog will not be pressure to eat unless he is hungry. This is true for several breeds of dogs. However, with an English Mastiff, controlling the amount of food that he consumes is difficult when he is free fed. English Mastiffs simply love to eat. So as long as there is food in the bowl, he will continue to eat and you will see your dog growing bigger and fatter with each passing day. The last thing you want to do is get a dog that is already that large to become obese.

What are the advantages of scheduled feeding?

• You do not have to worry about your dog eating till he is sick or obese.
• You can regulate what your dog is eating, how much he is eating and how often he is eating. That way, you have a direct control over his weight and health.
• Since your dog knows that it is you who decides when to feed him, he will also try consciously to be obedient to you and not upset you, thus, risking his next meal.

Can I go wrong with scheduled feeding?

Well, of course. There are some common mistakes that occur when you opt for scheduled feeding. You may, however, avoid these mistakes with a little bit of planning and information:
• You might forget to feed your dog sometimes.
• The amount of food in each serving might not be enough for the proper development of your English Mastiff
• The timing between two meals may be unequal, with some meals being too close and some being too far apart.
• Without proper training, your dog might become a little aggressive during the meal times when he knows his regular feeding timings.

Can the feeding method interfere with training?

There is no real evidence to suggest that free feeding or scheduled feeding have an impact on your dog's training. However, many pet owners and breeders believe that scheduled feeding works best when you are trying to housetrain your dog. Since you are feeding him at a certain time, he will also need to be taken out to relieve himself at a certain time. It is not that free feeding will lead to an undisciplined dog. However, it is certain that free feeding makes it harder for you to train your dog. Another thing that happens with free feeding is that your dog will no longer view food as a reward. Hence, you might not be able to use treats effectively as a reward for performing certain tasks correctly.

3. What to Feed my English Mastiff?

Like I mentioned before, there are several beliefs about feeding that vary from one owner to another. Whatever is mentioned in this book is based on my personal experiences with my Mastiffs. For some of you this might seem perfect while there may be some of you who might not find this suitable for your schedule or lifestyle. Irrespective of what you choose to feed your dog, the goal should be to ensure that he gets all the nutrition that he requires.

When you feed your dog only dry kibble, he will require between 4 to 6 pounds or 2 to 4 kilos of dry kibble each day. What works for me is combining dry kibble with home cooked meals. Different types of meats like chicken, mutton or pork can be cooked and mixed with the dry kibble. You may also add vegetables to this mixture to make the food more nutritious. Including a small amount of grains in his meal will also work really well. For this, you may make porridge with bran, wheat, brown rice or even oats and mix it with dry kibble and vegetables. While this is a broad overview of the foods that are suitable for an English Mastiff, there are certain specifications that you need to follow with every stage of growth of your English Mastiff.

For instance, many of us might believe that feeding an English Mastiff a high protein diet is the right thing to do when he is growing. However, after eight weeks of age, you must choose a dry kibble or a diet plan that is rich in carbohydrates and fats instead of proteins. This is because a high protein diet does not allow the skeletal system to form properly. When an English Mastiff is give a protein rich diet during the formative years, he will gain mass and grow very rapidly. The proportion of his body mass does not match with his skeletal development, leading to several problems.

The food that you choose for your English Mastiff has a lot of consequences. It has an impact on his temperament, his coat and also his health. While it is easy to get carried away with what will suit your dog the best, you must first understand the individual requirement of your English Mastiff before you proceed to fix a diet for him. You may consult your vet to give you suggestions and help you chalk out an age appropriate plan.

Feeding a puppy

The most obvious food for your English Mastiff when he is a puppy is the milk from his dam. It is instinctive for him to begin to suckle the moment he is born. If you have had an English Mastiff puppy birth in your home, you must watch if he suckles or not. If he does not start suckling within half an hour of his birth, you must place him on a nipple that has plenty of milk. When a puppy gets his mother's milk, he will get the most necessary colostrums that will keep him protected for the first eight to ten months of his life.

Undoubtedly, the dam's milk is the best thing for a puppy. However, if your puppy does not feed on the dam's milk, you must feed him yourself. There are several milk formulas that are available in the market. If you do not have enough experience, your veterinarian is the best person to help you give your puppy the best. The thing with feeding a puppy is that it is not good enough to just give him the right quantity of food. You must also choose the right quality of food for you puppy. For the first few days, you must feed your puppy at intervals of two hours.

The first six months are very important in for your puppy's feeding. He must be given his dam's milk for at least six weeks after he is born. It is from the third and fourth week that you start introducing him to solid foods. However, there are some breeders and pet owners who believe in providing solid foods earlier to build the puppy into the weaning stage. There are alternate milks and solid foods that are available for your puppy.

It is best to wean your puppy completely from the dam's milk by the time he is seven or eight weeks old. If you are unable to wean him off by this age, it will be difficult to get him to eat the right foods.

There are several junior and puppy foods that are available for your puppy. Be sure to keep the food completely balanced when your English Mastiff is in his growing years. Overfeeding him is just as bad as underfeeding him. The puppy must be fed to grow steadily and not too soon as he will develop skeletal and joint problems when he grows too big for his small frame.

Feeding an adult English Mastiff

You can give your English Mastiff the food necessary for an adult when he is about 3 months old. While a puppy should get not more than 24% of proteins in his diet, you can increase the proportions when your English Mastiff is older. When you are making this transition you must definitely consult your vet so that you are able to put your English Mastiff on a great maintenance diet.

There are major brands that you can opt for as they specialize in foods for large dogs like the English Mastiff. You must check the proportions of several nutrients present in these foods to choose something that is perfect for your English Mastiff. You must never simply choose a diet because a fellow English Mastiff owner is using a certain diet. Senior and adult dog diets vary as per the dog's body and the circumstances of the dog.

It is great to add some organ meet into the diet of your English Mastiff. Only about 10 % of the total diet should comprise of organ meat. Your English Mastiff will reach complete adulthood when he is about 2 years old. While some dogs mature fully by the time when they are 16 months old, some may take about three and a half years.

Feeding a Senior English Mastiff

As your English Mastiff grows older, his diet must also change. This is because his metabolism isn't the same as a younger English Mastiff. As your dog grows older, the amount of exercise that he gets will also come down significantly. He will also not be able to move as fast as a younger dog. He will also be more sedentary and will sleep for longer periods of time. As his physiology changes, his dietary requirement will also change. You must pay close attention to the development of your English Mastiff as the changes in his metabolism and his physiology take place so slowly that they may go unnoticed.

If you continue to feed him a regular adult dog's diet, he will begin to gain weight. This is because he will not be able metabolize the food as easily as when he was younger. As your dog grows old, he might have developed several health problems that are age dependant. If he is obese, these problems will only increase and become worse if you do not manage his diet properly.

Another change that you will notice is the deterioration of the function of his organs. The kidneys of your dogs will become less efficient and the intestines will not be able to function like before. You can take care of all these age related issues only when you change the diet of your English Mastiff with age. Make sure that your dog gets food that he will be able to digest easily. You may also have to reduce the portions of each meal as the dog grows older.

The change in the diet will depend upon your English Mastiff's health as he grows older. Sometimes, Mastiffs require a diet that is extremely light. On the other hand, if your English Mastiff is pretty healthy, he will do extremely well even on diets that are premium. Consult your English Mastiff's vet on every stage as he is the one who observes how your English Mastiff is performing internally as he is growing older.

With the right diet, you will be able to give your English Mastiff the perfect amount of vitamins, minerals and other nutrients that are necessary in keeping him healthy and good looking. If you want to present your English Mastiff in shows, you might have to take special care to provide supplements that will improve the quality of his foods. However, if you are including these supplements, make sure you check with your English Mastiff's vet first.

Give him enough water

For a dog as large as the English Mastiff, giving him ample water is a must to make sure that his large body has the opportunity to cool off. You must make sure that large amount of clean drinking water is always available for him to drink.

Water is just like all the nutrients that you include in the diet of your English Mastiff. In fact, it is probably more important as it helps your English Mastiff metabolize and make use of the nutrients that he is obtaining through the diet. Water is also necessary for his organs to function properly. If his body is not well hydrated, his organs might fail and have several problems.

With the English Mastiff, it is necessary to change the water in the bowl on a regular basis. This is because the English Mastiff tends to leave in a lot of slime in the water as he drools while drinking water. You may also require a special towel or cloth to wipe off the excessive food and water that drips and flies around thanks to his terribly loose dewlap. Otherwise, you must be prepared for the drool to be all over you as your English Mastiff will come to you any bury his head in your lap immediately after he has had a satisfying meal.

Choosing and storing food

Since there are several types of foods available for dogs, you might find it quite challenging to get the right and the most nutritious food for your English Mastiff. There is no fixed proportion to feed your English Mastiff. The best way to decide what is right for your English Mastiff is to give your dog feeding trials. Ask your vet to recommend the right food groups that you can include in the diet. These trials are dependent upon the weight, activity level and age of your dog. Once you find what is right for your English Mastiff, you may continue it for your English Mastiff.

You might see that your English Mastiff will enjoy certain flavors of food available in the market. While the taste of the food is not really a factor for your English Mastiff, he will be interested in the smell of the food! You can store different flavors to keep some novelty in the food that you give your English Mastiff.

Once you have purchased the foods that will be suitable for your English Mastiff, the next challenge is to ensure that the food is stored well. If you do not keep the foods tightly closed, all the nutrients will escape rendering the food entirely useless. When you are preparing home cooked meals for your English Mastiff, you can be sure of the freshness. However, of you are giving him store bought foods, close them securely and store them in a place where they are free from moisture and dust.

4. Feeding tips for an English Mastiff

There are some simple tips that will make it easier for your to feed your English Mastiff and ensure that you do not miss out on any of the basics.

•   The food that you serve your English Mastiff must never be too hot or too cold. Food that is in room temperature is best digested by your English Mastiff. Of course, for basic safety reasons you must try to give him food that is maintained at room temperature.

•   If you are giving your English Mastiff dry food, giving him enough water is a must. You must always serve the food of your English Mastiff with a bowl of clean and fresh water.

• Feeding your dog food from the table is not a good idea. Your English Mastiff must never give him leftovers from the food that you eat. These foods contain too much seasoning and fats that are not good for your English Mastiff.

• Chewing is a great habit for your dog's teeth to develop well. For this reason, giving him dry kibble or even meat chunks is a great idea as he will have to chew his food well. Giving him soups and stews is not recommended for your dog.

• The normal food or your dog must not be changed. This means, adding leftovers of your food or mixing in a new commercial food is not good for your English Mastiff. These foods add on to the normal diet and break the balance.

• You must change the diet of your English Mastiff only for age related reasons. Otherwise, giving him the same food everyday is the right way to go. Dogs don't get bored or sick of the same food over and over again.

With these simple tips, you can be assured that your English Mastiff will grow up with all the nutrients that he requires. He will be alert and will be able to function perfectly.

5. Poisonous Foods

While some dogs are smart enough not to want to eat foods that can harm or kill them, other canine companions will eat absolutely anything they can get their teeth on.

As conscientious guardians for our fur friends, it will always be our responsibility to make certain that when we share our homes with a dog, we never leave foods that could be toxic or lethal to them easily within their reach.

While there are many foods that can be toxic to a dog, the following alphabetical list contains some of the more common foods that can seriously harm or even kill our dogs including:

Bread Dough: if your dog eats bread dough, their body heat will cause the dough to rise inside the stomach. As the dough expands during the rising process, alcohol is produced.

Dogs who have eaten bread dough may experience stomach bloating, abdominal pain, vomiting, disorientation and depression. Because bread dough can rise to many times its original size, eating only a small amount will cause a problem for any dog.

Broccoli: the toxic ingredient in this food is isothiocynateyou're your dog eats broccoli, even though it will not be seriously harmful (unless more than 10% of the dog's normal daily diet is eaten), it will most likely cause stomach upset.

Chocolate: contains theobromine, a chemical that is toxic to dogs in large enough quantities. Chocolate also contains caffeine, which is found in coffee, tea, and certain soft drinks. Different types of chocolate contain different amounts of theobromine and caffeine.

For example, dark chocolate and baking chocolate or cocoa powder contain more of these compounds than milk chocolate does, therefore, a dog would need to eat more milk chocolate in order to become ill.

However, even a few ounces of chocolate can be enough to cause illness or death in a puppy or small dog therefore, no amount or type of chocolate should be considered safe for a dog to eat.

A dog suffering from having eaten chocolate may display symptoms that include diarrhea, vomiting, increased heart rate, restless behavior, muscle tremors, or seizures. If they have eaten enough of it, they could die within 24 hours of eating.

During many holidays such as Christmas, New Year's, Valentine's, Easter and Halloween, chocolate is often more easily accessible to curious dogs, especially from children who are not so careful with where they might keep their Halloween or Easter egg stash and who are an easy mark for a hungry dog

In some cases, people unwittingly poison their dogs by offering them chocolate as a treat or leaving chocolate cookies or frosted cake easily within licking distance.

Caffeine: beverages containing caffeine, such as soda, tea, coffee, and chocolate, act as a stimulant and can accelerate your dog's heartbeat to a dangerous level. Dogs eating caffeine have been known to have seizures, some of which are fatal.

Cooked Bones: can be extremely hazardous for a dog because when the bones are cooked, they become soft and can splinter when the dog chews on them.

A splintered piece of bone will usually have sharp edges that can easily become stuck in the teeth, puncture the gums, and cause choking if they get caught in the throat. If a sharp piece is swallowed, this could rupture or puncture the intestinal tract or stomach.

Especially dangerous are cooked chicken legs, cooked turkey legs, pork, ham and veal bones. Symptoms of choking include:

Pale or blue gums
Gasping breathing or panting
Pawing or scratching at the face
Slowed, shallow breathing
Collapse and unconsciousness with dilated pupils

Grapes and Raisins: can cause acute (sudden) kidney failure in dogs. While it is not known what the toxic agent is in this fruit, clinical signs can occur within 24 hours of eating these foods and include diarrhea, vomiting and tiredness.

Other signs of illness caused from eating grapes or raisins relate to the eventual shutdown of kidney functioning.

Garlic and Onions: contain chemicals that damage red blood cells by rupturing them so that they lose their ability to carry oxygen effectively, which leave the dog short of oxygen, causing what is called *"hemolytic anemia"*.

Poisoning can occur when a dog eats a large amount of garlic or onions all at once, or when eating repeated meals containing smaller amounts.

Cooking does not reduce the potential toxicity of onions and garlic.

NOTE: fresh, cooked, and/or powdered garlic or onions are commonly found in baby food, which is sometimes given to dogs when they are sick, therefore, be certain to carefully read food labels before feeding to your dog.

Macadamia Nuts: are commonly found in candies and chocolates. Although what causes macadamia nut toxicity is not well understood, the clinical signs in dogs having eaten these nuts may include depression, pale gums, weakness, vomiting, tremors and joint pain, which can occur approximately 12 hours after eating.

Sometimes symptoms can resolve themselves without treatment within 24 to 48 hours, however, keeping a close eye on your dog will be strongly recommended.

Mushrooms: mushroom poisoning can be fatal if certain species of mushrooms are eaten.

The most commonly reported severely toxic species of mushroom in the US is Amanita phalloides (Death Cap mushroom), which is also quite a common species found in most parts of Britain. Other Amanita species are also toxic.

This deadly mushroom is often found growing in grassy or wooded areas near various deciduous and coniferous trees, which mean that if you're out walking with your dog in the woods, they could easily find these mushrooms.

Eating them can cause severe liver disease and neurological disorders. If you suspect your dog has eaten these mushrooms, immediately take them to your veterinarian, as the recommended treatment is to induce vomiting and to give activated charcoal. Further treatment for liver disease may also be necessary.

Pits and Seeds: many seeds and pits found in a variety of fruits, including apples, apricots, cherries, pears and plums, contain cyanogenic glycosides that can cause cyanide poisoning in your dog.

The symptoms of cyanide poisoning usually occur within 15-20 minutes to a few hours after eating and symptoms can include initial excitement, followed by rapid respiration rate, salivation, voiding of urine and feces, vomiting, muscle spasm, staggering, and coma before death.

Dogs suffering from cyanide poisoning that live more than 2 hours after onset of symptoms will usually recover.

Raw Salmon or Trout: Salmon Poisoning Disease (SPD) can be a problem for anyone who goes fishing with their dog, or feeds their dog a raw meat diet that includes raw salmon or trout.
When a snail is infected and then is eaten by the fish, as part of the food chain, the dog is exposed when it eats the infected fish.

A sudden onset of symptoms can occur 5-7 days after eating the infected fish. In the acute stages, gastrointestinal symptoms are quite similar to canine parvovirus.

SPD has a mortality rate of up to 90%, can be diagnosed with a fecal sample and is treatable if caught in time.

Prevention is simple, cook all fish before feeding it to your dog and immediately see your veterinarian if you suspect that your dog has eaten raw salmon or trout.

Tobacco: all forms of tobacco, including patches, nicotine gum and chewing tobacco can be fatal to dogs if eaten.

Signs of poisoning can appear quite rapidly (within an hour or less) and may include diarrhea, vomiting, a heightened state of activity, excessive salivating and panting.

Depending upon how much a dog may have eaten, more acute signs of poisoning may cause twitching, leading to collapse and coma due to heart attack that will cause death.

Never leave tobacco products within reach of your dog, and be careful not to let them pick up discarded cigarette butts when they are young puppies.
If you suspect your dog has eaten any of these, seek immediate veterinary help.

TIP: when your dog is a very young puppy, use a double leash, collar and harness arrangement, so that you can still teach them to walk on leash with a Martingale collar around their neck, but can also attach the second leash to their harness so that you can easily lift them over enticing cigarette butts or other toxic garbage they may be trying to eat during your walks.

Tomatoes: there is atropine in tomatoes, which can cause tremors, dilated pupils, tremors and an irregular heartbeat in a dog that eats them. The greatest amount of atropine will be found in the stalks and leaves of the tomato plant, next is the green tomato (before it ripens), and then ripe tomatoes.

Xylitol: is a highly used artificial sweetener, which is often an ingredient in candy, gum, breath mints, toothpaste and mouthwash that is recognized by the National Animal Poison Control Center to be a risk to dogs.

When dogs eat products containing Xylitol, it causes a sudden release of insulin, which causes low blood sugar, which can also cause liver damage.

Within 30 minutes after eating a product containing Xylitol, the dog may vomit, appear to be tired, and/or be uncoordinated. However, some signs of toxicity can also be delayed for hours or even for a few days. Xylitol toxicity in dogs can be fatal if left untreated.

Please be aware that the above list is just some of the more common foods that can be toxic or fatal to our fur friends and that there are many other foods we should never be feeding our dogs.

If you have one of those dogs who will happily eat anything that looks or smells even slightly like food, be certain to keep these foods far away from your beloved dog and you'll help them to live a long and healthy life.

6. Poisonous Household Plants

Many common house plants are actually poisonous to our canine companions, and although many dogs simply will ignore house plants, some will attempt to eat anything, especially puppies who want to taste everything in their new world.

More than 700 plant species contain toxins that may harm or be fatal to puppies or dogs, depending on the size of the puppy or dog and how much they may eat. It will be especially important to be aware of household plants that could be toxic when you are sharing your home with a new puppy.

Following is a short list of the more common household plants, what they look like, the different names they are known by, and what symptoms would be apparent if your puppy or dog decides to eat them.

Aloe Plant: also known as *"medicine plant or Barbados aloe"*, is a very common succulent plant that is toxic to dogs. The toxic agent in this plant is Aloin.

This bitter yellow substance is found in most aloe species and may cause vomiting and/or reddish urine.

Asparagus Fern: is also known as *"lace fern, emerald fern, emerald feather, sprengeri fern and plumosa fern"*. The toxic agent in this plant is sapogenin, which is a steroid found in a variety of plants. Repeated exposure to the berries of this plant cause vomiting, diarrhea and/or abdominal pain or skin inflammation.

Corn Plant: also known as *"ribbon plant, cornstalk plant, dragon tree and dracaena"*, is toxic to dogs. Saponin is the offensive chemical compound found in this plant. If the plant is eaten, vomiting (with or without blood), loss of appetite, depression and/or increased drooling can occur.

Cyclamen: also known as *"Sowbread"*, is a pretty, flowering plant that, if eaten, can cause diarrhea, vomiting and increased salivation. If a dog eats a large amount of the plant's tubers, usually found underneath the soil at the root level, heart rhythm problems can occur, which may result in seizures or even death.

Dieffenbachia: also known as *"exotica, dumb cane and tropic snow"* contains a chemical that is a poisonous deterrent to animals. If a dog eats the plant, they will experience mouth irritation, especially on the tongue and lips that can lead to increased drooling, problems swallowing and vomiting.

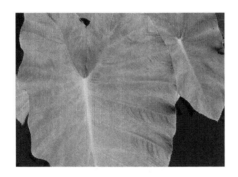

Elephant Ear: also known as *"cape, caladium, malanga, pai, taro and via sori,"* contains a chemical which is similar to a chemical also found in dieffenbachia. A dog's toxic reaction to elephant ear is similar, including oral irritation, problems swallowing, increased drooling, and vomiting.

Heartleaf Philodendron: also known as "cordatum, split-leaf philodendron, fiddle leaf, fruit salad plant, horsehead philodendron, panda plant, red emerald, red princess, and saddle leaf", is a very common, easy-to-grow houseplant that contains a chemical irritating to the mouth, tongue and lips of dogs. An affected dog may also experience difficulty swallowing, vomiting and increased drooling.

Jade Plant: has many other names, including "baby jade, Chinese rubber plant, dwarf rubber plant, friendship tree, jade tree, or Japanese rubber plant". While exactly what is toxic to dogs in this plant is unknown, a dog eating a Jade plant can suffer from loss of coordination and depression as well as a slowed heart rate.

Lilies: some plants of the lily family can be toxic to dogs. The peace lily (also known as Mauna Loa) is known to be toxic to dogs. Eating the peace lily or calla lily can cause vomiting, irritation to the dog's tongue and lips, problems swallowing and increased drooling.

Satin Pothos: (silk pothos), if eaten by a dog, the plant may cause irritation to the dog's mouth, lips and tongue, while the dog may also experience vomiting, difficulty swallowing and drooling.

The plants noted above are only a few of the more common household plants, and every conscientious dog guardian will want to educate themselves before bringing plants into the home that could be toxic to their canine companions.

7. Poison Proof Your Home

You can learn about many potentially toxic and poisonous sources both inside and outside your home by visiting the ASPCA Animal Poison Control Center website.

Always keep your veterinarian's emergency number in a place where you can quickly access it, as well as the Emergency Poison Control telephone number, in case you suspect that your dog may have been poisoned.

Knowing what to do if you suspect your dog may have been poisoned and being able to quickly contact the right people could save your dog's life.

If you keep toxic cleaning substances (including fertilizers, vermin or snail poisons and vehicle products) in your home or garage, always keep them behind closed doors.

As well, keep any medications where your dog can never get to them, and seriously consider eliminating the use of any and all toxic products, for the health of both yourself and your best friend.

8. Garden Plants

Please note that there are also many outdoor plants that can be toxic or poisonous to your dog, therefore, always check what plants are growing in your garden and if any may be harmful, remove them or make certain that your puppy or adult dog cannot eat them.

Cornell University, Department of Animal Science lists many different categories of poisonous plants affecting dogs, including house plants, flower garden plants, vegetable garden plants, plants found in swamps or moist areas, plants found in fields, trees and shrubs, plants found in wooded areas, and ornamental plants.

9. Why Does My Dog Eat Grass?

Also, be aware that many puppies and adult dogs will eat grass, just because. Perhaps they are curious, bored, or need a little fiber in their diet.

Remember that canines are natural scavengers always on the lookout for something they can eat, and so long as the grass is healthy and has not been sprayed with toxic chemicals, this should not be a concern.

10. Animal Poison Control Centre

The ASPCA Animal Poison Control Center is staffed 24 hours a day, 365 days a year and is a valuable resource for learning about what plants are toxic and possibly poisonous to your dog.

a) USA Poison Emergency

Call: 1 (888) 426-4435

When calling the Poison Emergency number, your credit card may be charged with a $65. ((£39.42) consultation fee.

b) UK Poison Emergency

Call: 0800-213-6680 - Pet Poison Helpline (payable service)

Call: 0300 1234 999 - RSPCA

www.aspca.org = ASPCA Poison Control.

Chapter 11: Grooming Your English Mastiff

Grooming your English Mastiff is more than just making him look good. You need to groom your dog in order to ensure that he remains healthy and clean. If you ignore the basic grooming rituals, there are several infections that might be on their way. Grooming is also needed to take care of certain safety standards. For instance, clipping of the nails is essential to ensure that he English Mastiff does not hurt himself or others.

Brushing your English Mastiff

Brushing is a routine grooming activity that is essential for your English Mastiff's fur. There are several kinds of brushes available in the market that work perfectly on your English Mastiff's short and rough hair. Choose a brush that reaches down to the skin of your English Mastiff so that he gets a good and thorough brushing.

Brushing is more than just an activity that keeps your English Mastiff's fur looking good. It is a very practical grooming routine for several reasons such as:

• All the dead skin and hair that accumulates on your English Mastiff's body is removed. This helps keep the pores unclogged and also prevents the hair from shedding all over your house.

• Brushing the hair with even strokes also improves blood circulation making it easier for the new skin and fur to grow.

119

- Brushing is a great opportunity for you to check for bumps and rashes that may go unnoticed when you don't pay attention to the skin of the English Mastiff.

- Grooming and brushing the hair is a great way for you to bond with your English Mastiff.

Brushing the hair at least twice a week is highly recommended. The short and rough fur of your English Mastiff is not exactly high maintenance but a good brushing session impacts the overall hygiene of your dog. Unlike bathing brushing is an activity that y our English Mastiff will also enjoy thoroughly. If you use even and smooth strokes, to brush your English Mastiff's fur it will feel like a day at the spa for your beloved pet.

Bathing

Bathing a dog is something that every pet owner and pet finds stressful. The issue with most pets is that they are not given a regular bathing routine from the time they are puppies. If you train your English Mastiff to expect a bath after a certain interval you will notice that he will struggle and fuss a lot lesser.

A dog does not require a bath as often as people. However, a good bath at regular intervals is a must. With the dogs like an English Mastiff that has so many wrinkles on his body bathing him becomes a lot more necessary. There are several areas where dirt and germs can accumulate and cause serious infections. So you must make sure that you give him a bath that is thorough. Follow the steps below to ensure that your English Mastiff is getting the right kind of bath:

- Step 1: Wet the fur of your English Mastiff completely. You may use a water hose for a Mastiff that is fully grown.

- Step 2: Use a good dog shampoo and work up a lather. Always shampoo the body first, wash it and then proceed to the face. When you are shampooing your English Mastiff make sure that you get the shampoo well into the skin. While you are doing so be on the lookout for bumps, boils or lesions in the skin.

• Step 3: As mentioned before rinse the body and wash it thoroughly and wash the shampoo out thoroughly before proceeding to his face. When you wash the face of the English Mastiff direct the water away from his eyes. If you are washing his forehead cover his eyes with your hand.

• Step 4: Your English Mastiff will start this step for you by shaking off the water vigorously. So after you have rinsed your English Mastiff, use a leash or collar to step away from him while still having a firm grip. This prevents your English Mastiff from running away. Once he has done his bit use a large and heavy towel to remove all they excess water. If it is a warm and sunny day allow his coat to dry naturally. However, if the weather is cold use a hair dryer.

When you are bathing your English Mastiff there are some safety precautions that you need to take. If you are bathing a puppy, you would probably use a basin or a tub. Make sure you have a non slippery surface made of rubber or cement to prevent injuries. Never use shampoo that is meant for human hair. These shampoos are too abrasive in nature and will strip off the essential oils from the skin of the English Mastiff. There are specially formulated dog soaps that are available in all pet stores. Your Vet will also be able to provide you with medicated shampoos that are good for your English Mastiff's skin. Always make sure that you rinse the fur completely and get rid of all the shampoo. If you leave the shampoo behind, even traces of it, the chemicals in them can lead to skin infections.

Sometimes, your English Mastiff may require some spot fixing. In such cases you have dry shampoos and dry bathing products that are available in the form of sprays and powders. Although these are not replacements for a regular bath, you can use them when your English Mastiff decides to get a little messy.

When you give your English Mastiff a bath always try to keep him relaxed. Take a lot of time out to give him a bath so that you don't end up rushing things. Talk to him soothingly and give him some of his favorite toys so that he remains distracted. The best thing to do is to make him associate bathing time with fun and other positive emotions right from his first bath.

Cleaning your English Mastiff's ears

The ears are the most sensitive part on a dog's head. It is prone to infections that might have serious repercussions on the overall health of your English Mastiff; Taking complete care of the ears is your prime responsibility as the owner.
You can use cotton swabs or ear buds to get into the deeper areas of the ear. You need to be very gentle as you may damage the inner ear if you are too rough. There are also special ear wipes that are available in pet stores to clean the ear as well as disinfect it. This is something that I strongly recommend for you to buy and store.

Another problem with the ear is that there may be some growth on the fur on the inside of the ear. If this ear hair is too dense parasites get an opportunity to hide and infect the area. Using small scissors and clipping the ear hair is strongly recommended for all dogs.

When you are cleaning the ear of an English Mastiff also check the ear for infections. If there is any redness or visible irritation of the skin you can be sure that it is an infection. Sometimes you can also smell an odd odor coming from the ears. This is a sure shot sign of ear mite infections in the ear. If you also notice that the English Mastiff is shaking its head too often or scratching his ears all the time, a thorough ear inspection is necessary.

Clipping the nails

When your dog is just walking down your hallway and you hear an obvious clicking sound coming from his toes it is a sign that your dog's nail needs clipping. Keeping the nails short makes your English Mastiff look smart and well groomed. Besides that there are three prime reasons for you to include nail clipping as a mandate in your English Mastiff's grooming routine:

• If the nails are too long they are at the risk of breaking and bleeding. If the nail breakage is too severe it might lead to limping in your English Mastiff.

• Someone might get injured when your English Mastiff playfully jumps on them or whacks them with his paw.

• All your sofas, rugs and carpets are at the risk of being damaged.

When you are cutting the nails of an English Mastiff be sensitive to a part known as the "Quick". The Quick is a blood vessel that goes almost till the tip of your English Mastiff's tail. This quick is visible when your dog has light colored nails. However if the nails are dark you must be extra careful when you are clipping the nails of your English Mastiff.

Sometimes it is possible that you accidently clip this Quick. This will lead to profuse bleeding and will be painful for your English Mastiff. So whenever you are clipping your English Mastiff's nails keep some cotton and coagulant handy. If you happen to cut the nail too far don't panic. Just apply some coagulant, stroke your dog and talk to him soothingly. When he has calmed down proceed to the next nail.

Whenever you are clipping the nails of your English Mastiff make sure you have a firm grip on him. This is especially important for puppies as they may make some quick movement or try to run away leading to injury. As for the adult English Mastiff I have found it very useful to gently clip his nails when he is asleep. Remember the state of slumber that I spoke to you about when an English Mastiff starts to snore? Plan all the nail clipping for then.

Always clip the nail little bit at a time. When the nail has reached the size that you are comfortable with simply file it to keep it well maintained. There are special dog nail clippers that help you cut your English Mastiff's nails quickly and safely.

Grooming a dog requires a great a deal of patience. Some activities like nail clipping and ear cleaning requires experience. If you are unsure about them you can hire dog grooming specialists to help you out and teach you the right way to keep your English Mastiff looking good safely and without any stress.

Although these services might be expensive in the beginning I recommend that you opt for them till you are able to care for your English Mastiff on your own.

Essentials for a grooming kit

When you are grooming your English Mastiff you must have all the things that are necessary to complete each grooming activity successfully. You must always update your kit and keep refilling things to ensure that you do not have run to and fro in the middle of a grooming session. Imagine a situation when you have taken your English Mastiff to the garden, wet his coat completely only to realize that you have run out of shampoo. All you will have is a wet and very displeased dog. To avoid these situations make sure your grooming kit has the following items:

- A good quality dog shampoo
- Pet hand gloves
- Brushes for the fur
- A dog hose
- Large Towel

- Tissues and wipes
- Cotton
- Blood coagulants
- Flee powder
- Dog nail trimmer
- A pair of small scissors

These are the basics. However you may add other things to this kit depending on your English Mastiff's requirements.

Chapter 12: Training Your English Mastiff

With a dog that is as large as an English Mastiff you must make sure that he is well trained. A dog his size is a huge responsibility and if he displays unacceptable behavior you may be putting around you and yourself at risk. Having a trained dog is also important because it is fun. If you have a dog that can respond the way you want him to it becomes easier to play with him and have a good time with him. Training a dog also gives you an opportunity to understand his communication and respond to it adequately.

If you are experienced with a big dog like an English Mastiff you may train him yourself. However, this is your first time it is a good idea to join an obedience class. You must teach your dog good manners and understand from where some behavioral pattern is coming from. Being able to communicate with your dog is a gift. It helps you understand that your pet is an interesting creature that is smart, well behaved and loads of fun. Training him also a great stress reliever for you. When you see your dog display his devotion to you on a daily basis, it is hugely rewarding. Every time your dog obeys you he treats you not just like a leader but considers you his hero. This works very well for a person's ego.

There are certain patterns that owners and obedience counselors have discovered in training and dog ownership. For instance, irrespective of the breed the best time to train a dog for maximum results and highest success rate is when he is a puppy. I am sure you have all heard of the saying "you cannot teach old dog new tricks". This saying is quite literal in its meaning. So if you want to exploit your dog's learning capability to its maximum you must ensure that you start right.

The best time to start training the puppy is when he is between 10 to 16 weeks old. During this time your puppy is highly curious and is able to learn about anything you teach him. At this stage you have one big advantage. Your dog is not producing any hormones. So training him ensures highest success rate. Until his hormones kick in is level of focus is very high and his point of focus is you. All he knows is that you are his source of food and security.

At this point all he wants to do is follow you from one room to another. He does not want you to be out of sight for even a moment. This is when an English Mastiff learns how to respond to other people and animals from you. If you are friendly he will be friendly. On the other hand if you are hesitant he would also be hesitant.

The next stage is when your English Mastiff begins to produce hormones. This is when he wants to understand what is around him. He will start investigating and exploring everything he sees. Hence his span of attention is extremely low. He will not be able to focus on you and listen to your commands. If you have not trained him as yet be prepared for an English Mastiff who will simply ignore your commands and wander away.

So when you know the time is right look for obedience classes near you. Sometimes the class may be close to your place but too expensive. If the class is reasonable the travelling time may be too much. So to make it easier for you I have put together certain procedures that will yield positive results. Age is not a barrier if you are patient and if you follow the right techniques of teaching and training. The most important thing to keep in mind is that you must use encouragement, motivation and applause as your biggest strengths while training your English Mastiff.

1. Housebreaking

If you don't want to run after your English Mastiff with a rag and a broom house breaking is the first thing you must teach him. It is very important to make it clear to your English Mastiff that there are only certain places that are suitable for him to use to relieve himself. In the beginning when you are just taking your puppy out to public places he may not be able to understand this command immediately. So until the house breaking is complete always carry a poop scoop with you to remove the droppings of your canine from public places.

There are two types of training that all dogs go through. One is outdoor training where surfaces cement and grass are involved. The other is the indoor training which involves your home. When you begin the house breaking process for your English Mastiff, decide where you want him to relieve himself. And this place should be permanent. If it is a sand box in your home make sure that you are sure about it. While sand boxes and indoor training works very well with cats for any dog outdoor house breaking is recommended.

For every habit that you need to teach, you must find a voice command that will initiate a habit. Now if you want your puppy to relieve himself using commands like "let us go, it's time to go, potty time etc." are commonly used. Every time you take your puppy out give him the relief command that you choose. When he grows into an adult, his behavior will tell you whether he wants to go or not. If he wags his tail, looks at you intently, runs to the door or shows any other sign of interest it means that he wants to go out.

When he is a puppy your English Mastiff will want to relieve himself after every meal and after every play session. You will usually see him looking around for a place to do his business. You see when an English Mastiff is a puppy the muscles in his urinary and intestinal tracts are not completely developed. So he needs to relieve himself quite frequently. Until he is older you will have to take him out every hour or after every meal and nap. As he grows older the number of times he needs to go out will reduce. When he is a mature and healthy adult he will not require more than 5 trips. Here is a simple chart that will tell you how many times your English Mastiff needs to go out.

- Up to 14 weeks : 10 times
- 14 to 22 weeks : 8 times
- 22 to 32 weeks : 6 times
- Adulthood   : 4 times

These numbers tell you the minimum relief sessions that your English Mastiff requires. However, depending upon the health and condition of your English Mastiff these numbers may vary.

Generally speaking, while your puppy is still growing, a young puppy can hold it approximately one hour for every month of their age.

This means that if your 2-month-old puppy has been happily snoozing for a couple of hours, as soon as they wake up, they will need to go outside.

Some of the first indications or signs that your puppy needs to be taken outside to relieve themselves will be when you see them:

- Sniffing around
- Circling
- Looking for or approaching the door
- Whining, crying or barking
- Acting agitated

a) Housing needs of a English Mastiff
With any puppy that you bring home you must establish some boundaries and take some control. Using different types of housing will teach your English Mastiff that there is a certain part of the house that belongs entirely to him while the rest of the house is a space that he shares with you and your family.

To establish this control you must first find that area that you can give to him entirely. This is the place where he will sleep, eat and

129

play. It is best that you choose a room where your family spends a good amount of time. A dog must always feel that he is a part of your family and must frequently hear your voice and see you walking about. The best places are the breakfast area in your kitchen, the family room or your bedroom.

In the room that you choose you can place a crate or create a gated corner that will become his territory. No matter what type of enclosure you choose, give size a lot of importance. He must be able to stretch well, play and be comfortable. You must ensure that the space is not so large that he can relieve himself at one end and comfortably rest at the other end. Dogs do not like to come in contact with their droppings. This is a also motivation for him to go outside and relieve himself. The enclosure must be lined with clean bedding. Make sure that water is always available and that his toys are always at an arm's length. One thing you must always keep in mind is that you should never put paper in his relieving area or on the floor while house training. If your puppy understands that you will pick up his droppings when he voids on a paper he will associate every paper with voiding. If your goal is to take your puppy outside he must be forced to go outside and do his business.

b) Take the lead

When you have a baby in the house you try to teach him your way of life. This is exactly what you must do with your English Mastiff. Take the lead and help him develop a lifestyle that fits in with you and your family's lifestyle. Your puppy must know when he should eat, when he should go out and exercise, when he should relieve himself and also when he can play.

Teach your puppy that he must sleep in his enclosure. He must also be trained to stay in his enclosure when your family is preparing for the day or when there is a lot of human activity in your home. When you leave the house the puppy must know where his area of safety is. Remember that making his enclosure a favorite space for him you will also prevent him from damaging your things. Instinctively English Mastiff loves to chew. They will chew on everything like shoes, furniture to wires. While chewing on furniture is nothing more than a mere damage of property, chewing a wire may be fatal to your English Mastiff. Also when you get back home and find your favorite shoe chewed into bits you may reprimand him for this act. Your English Mastiff does not even remember chewing on the shoe and will simply associate your coming back home to being punished. If you don't want this to happen train him to be in his enclosure.

Another advantage of giving your English Mastiff his own space is that he will be able to watch parties and gatherings without being fed with tit bits that may cause unwanted illnesses. He will not be under any stress but will still feel like being a part of all the fun.

c) Prepare a schedule

Every time you release your puppy from his designated area, finish a play session or give him a meal, take him out to the relief area. As he grows your puppy will show you signs himself. He will circle around the room, scratch the door or just sniff around. Until he knows to do this you must prepare a schedule.

Whenever you take him out of the relief area do not stay there for more than five to six minutes. Return to the house after this time period. If your puppy goes when you take him to the relief area, shower him with praise. On the other hand if he comes back home and then has an accident sharply say "No" and take him back to the relief area. Keep him there for a few minutes and come back. Never hit your puppy or scare him if he has an accident. Once you come back home keep him in his crate and clean up his mess. After that release him to play. If your puppy repeatedly misses going in his relief area chances are that your scheduling is wrong or that you do not understand his signs of wanting to go out. It is very important for you to make your puppy understand that going outdoor means relieving himself. When he is trained properly he will be able to tell the difference between playing and relief time. You must also provide similar scheduling for all activities like eating, napping etc. He must be trained to do all this in his enclosure while he is indoors. You must also teach your puppy to be b y himself. He needs to understand that you also have other activities to attend to apart from him.

Crate training is highly important for you to give your puppy a place when you know that he is safe. There is no short cut to crate training and house breaking. There are five things that you must ensure for maximum results:

- Frequency
- Consistency
- Control
- Praise
- Supervision

If you can follow these simple steps you will be able to house train your puppy successfully so that he can be a part of your life style and family.

d) Bell Training

A very easy way to introduce your new puppy to house training is to begin by teaching them how to ring a doorbell whenever they need to go outside.

Ringing a doorbell is not only a convenient alert system for both you and your puppy or dog, your visitors will be most impressed by how smart your dog is.

A further benefit of training your puppy to ring a bell is that you will not have to listen to your puppy or dog whining, barking or howling to be let out, and your door will not become scratched up from their nails.

Unless you prefer to purchase an already manufactured doggy doorbell or system, take a trip to your local novelty store and purchase a small bell that has a nice, loud ring.

Attach the bell to a piece of ribbon or string and hang it from a door handle or tape it to a door sill near the door where you will be taking your puppy out when they need to relieve themselves. The string will need to be long enough so that your puppy can easily reach the bell with their nose or a paw.

Next, each time you take your puppy out to go potty, say the word *"Out"*, and use their paw or their nose to ring the bell. Praise them for this *"trick"* and immediately take them outside.

The only down side to teaching your puppy or dog to ring a bell when they want to go outside, is that even if they don't actually have to go out to relieve themselves, but just want to go outside because they are bored, you will still have to take them out every time they ring the bell.

There are many types and styles of *"gotta go"* commercially manufactured bells you could choose, ranging from the elegant **"Poochie Bells™"** that hang from a doorknob, the simple **"Tell Bell™"** that sits on the floor, or various high tech door chime systems that function much like a doggy intercom system where they push a pad with their paw and it rings a bell. www.tellbell.com www.poochie-pets.net In the UK, these bells are available on www.amazon.co.uk

Whatever doorbell system you choose for your puppy, once they are trained, this type of an alert system is an easy way to eliminate accidents in the home.

e) Kennel Training
Kennel training is always a good idea for any puppy early in their education, because it can be utilized for many different situations, including keeping them safe while traveling inside a vehicle and being a very helpful tool for house training.

When purchasing a kennel for your puppy, always buy a kennel that will be the correct size for your puppy once they become an adult.

The kennel will be the correct size if an adult dog can stand up and easily turn around inside their kennel.

When you train your puppy to accept sleeping in their own kennel at nighttime, this will also help to accelerate their potty training, because no puppy or dog wants to relieve themselves where they sleep, which means that they will hold their bladder and bowels as long as they possibly can.

Always be kind and compassionate and remember that a puppy will be able to hold it approximately one hour for every month of their age.

Generally, a puppy that is three months old will be able to hold it for approximately three hours, unless they just ate a meal or had a big drink of water.

Be watchful and consistent so that you learn your puppy's body language, which will alert you to when it's time for them to go outside.

Presenting them with familiar scents, by taking them to the same spot in the yard or the same street corner, will help to remind and encourage them that they are outside to relieve themselves.

Use a voice cue to remind your puppy why they are outside, such as *"go pee"* and always remember to praise them every time they relieve themselves in the right place so that they quickly understand what you expect of them and will learn to *"go"* on cue.

f) Exercise Pen Training
The exercise pen is a transition from kennel only training and will be helpful for those times when you may have to leave your puppy for more hours than they can reasonably be expected to hold it.

During those times when you must be away from the home for several hours, it's time to introduce your puppy to an exercise pen.

Exercise pens are usually constructed of wire sections that you can put together in whatever shape you desire, and the pen needs to be large enough to hold your puppy's kennel inside one half of the pen, while the other half will be lined with newspapers or pee pads.

Place your puppy's food and water dishes next to the kennel and leave the kennel door open, so they can wander in and out whenever they wish, to eat or drink or go to the papers or pads if they need to relieve themselves.

Your puppy will be contained in a small area of your home while you are away and because they are already used to sleeping inside their kennel, they will not want to relieve themselves inside the area where they sleep. Therefore, your puppy will naturally go to the other half of the pen to relieve themselves on the newspapers or pee pads.

This method will help train your puppy to be quickly "paper" trained when you must leave them alone for a few hours.

g) Puppy Apartment™ Training

A similar and more costly alternative, the *Puppy Apartment™* is a step up from the exercise pen training system that makes the process of crate or pen training even easier on both humans and puppies.

The Puppy Apartment™ works well in a variety of situations, whether you're at home and unable to pay close attention to your puppy's needs, whether you must be away from the home for a few hours or during the evening when everyone is asleep and you don't particularly want to get up at 3:00 a.m. to take your puppy out to go pee.

135

The Puppy Apartment™ is an innovation that is convenient for both puppy and human alike.

What makes this system so effective is the patent pending dividing wall with a door leading to the other side, all inside the pen.

One side of the Puppy Apartment™ is where the puppy's bed is located and the other side (through the doorway) is the bathroom area that is lined with pee pads.

With the bathroom right next door, your puppy or dog can take a bathroom break whenever they wish, without the need to alert family members to let them out.

This one bedroom, one bathroom system, which is a combination of the kennel/training pen, is a great alternative for helping to eliminate the stress of worrying about always keeping a watchful eye on your puppy or getting up during the night to take them outside every few hours to help them avoid making mistakes.

According to Modern Puppies: *"The Puppy Apartment™ takes the MESSY out of paper training, the ODORS AND HASSLES out of artificial grass training, MISSING THE MARK out of potty pad training and HAVING TO HOLD IT out of crate training. House training a puppy has never been faster or easier! The Puppy Apartment™ has taken all the benefits of the most popular potty training methods and combined them into one magical device and potty training system. This device and system has revolutionized how modern puppies are potty trained!"*

Manufactured in the United States, this product ships directly from the California supplier (Modern Puppies).

Pricing of the Puppy Apartment™ begins at $138. USD (£83.37) and is only available online at Modern Puppies.

h) Free Training

If you would rather not confine your young puppy to one or two rooms in your home, and will be allowing them to freely range about your home anywhere they wish during the day, this is considered free training.

When free house training your puppy, you will need to closely watch your puppy's activities all day long so that you can be aware of the *"signs"* that will indicate when they need to go outside to relieve themselves.

For instance, circling and sniffing is a sure sign that they are looking for a place to do their business.

Never get upset or scold a puppy for having an accident inside the home, because this will result in teaching your puppy to be afraid of you and to only relieve themselves in secret places or when you're not watching.

If you catch your puppy making a mistake, all that is necessary is for you to calmly say *"No"*, and quickly scoop them up and take them outside or to their indoor bathroom area.

From your sensitive puppy's point of view, yelling or screaming when they make a potty mistake, will be understood by your puppy or dog as unstable energy being displayed by the person who is supposed to be their leader. This type of unstable behavior will only teach your puppy to fear and disrespect you.

When you are vigilant, your puppy should not a difficult puppy to housebreak and they will generally do very well when you start them off with *"puppy pee pads"* that you will move closer and closer to the same door that you always use when taking them outside. This way they will quickly learn to associate going to this door when they need to relieve themselves.

When you pay close attention to your puppy's sleeping, eating, drinking and playing habits, you will quickly learn their body language so that you are able to predict when they might need to relieve themselves.

Your puppy will always need to relieve themselves first thing in the morning, as soon as they wake up from a nap, approximately 20 minutes after they finish eating a meal, after they have finished a play session, and of course, before they go to bed at night.

It's important to have compassion during this house training time in your young puppy's life so that their education will be as stress-free as possible.

It's also important to be vigilant because how well you pay attention will minimize the opportunities your puppy may have for making a bathroom mistake in the first place, and the fewer mistakes they make, the sooner your puppy will be house trained.

i) Mistakes Happen
Remember that a dog's sense of smell is at least 2,000 times more sensitive that our human sense of smell.

As a result of your puppy's superior sense of smell, it will be very important to effectively remove all odors from house training accidents, because otherwise, your puppy will be attracted by the smell to the place where they may have had a previous accident, and will want to do their business there again and again.

While there are many products that are supposed to remove odors and stains, many of these are not very effective. You want a professional grade cleaner that will not just mask one odor with another scent, you want a product that will completely neutralize odors.

TIP: go to RemoveUrineOdors.com and order yourself some *"SUN"* and/or *"Max Enzyme"* because these products contain professional-strength odor neutralizers and urine digesters that bind to and completely absorb odors on any type of surface.

2. The Effect of Reward, Punishment and Discipline

Any social animal whether it is a dog or a human being requires discipline to function effectively in a group. In simple terms discipline is nothing but acting in accordance to certain rules. These rules may vary from one family to another but are essential to avoid chaos. Domestic canines must be disciplined in order to be able to function like their own pack which is you and your family. They must be taught that there is a certain way to behave if they want to survive in this group.

In a recently conducted survey it was observed that dog owners who had well trained dogs were 75% more satisfied than those who had never trained dogs. The two things that we use to teach a dog how to behave. They are rewards and punishments.

In order to understand which one is better than the other, let us take a look at *Thorndike's theory of learning* which was established by Dr Edward Thorndike, a noted psychologist. According to him any behavior that ends in a positive event will be repeated. Similarly a behavior that ends with a negative event will never be repeated. All training methods we use today are based on this theory. For instance, when your dog performs certain activity that you approve of give him a reward. This will make him repeat that activity. Sometimes negative reinforcements may become necessary. However it is best that a negative reinforcement comes from an outside source. For instance, you may have repeatedly told your dog to stop teasing the cat in your house. However, he continues to disobey you and chases the cat. Eventually the cat will try to defend himself and swipe a claw across his face. This painful gash is the unpleasant event that will prevent your dog from repeating the act.

3. Equipment Required for Training

• Collar and lead: When you are training your English Mastiff use a collar and lead that is not very heavy but sturdy enough to hold him back. The collar and the lead give you that position of authority which will ensure that your dog knows who the leader is.

• Treats: Give your English Mastiff loads of treats when you are training your English Mastiff. Keep something that you know is very easy to swallow. A soft treat that your dog can eat immediately is recommended. If you give a dog a hard treat he will forget what he is being rewarded for by the time he finishes chewing his treat. When you do this your English Mastiff will associate treats with praise and will repeat behavior that helped him earn the treat.

4. Basic Commands to Teach your English Mastiff

There are some simple things that you must do when you start teaching your English Mastiff some basic commands. The most important of all these things is the voice command or the question. Before you train a dog you must get his attention first. If your English Mastiff's mind is on something else and he is busy looking elsewhere he will never learn anything. When you start training use the words such as "school" in an excited voice. That will grab his attention and he will walk towards you. Give him a treat and praise him. Repeat this routine a couple of more times. By the third time your dog will understand that paying attention to you will get him a treat. Basically he associates the word "school" with fun. This technique applies to every trick that you will teach your dog.

A dog does not understand our language. So he is only responding to the sounds that you are making and the tone of a particular sound. These sounds are the commands that your dog is responding to. There are a few basic voice commands that all dogs need to know.

a) Teaching your dog to sit
First get your English Mastiff's attention and make sure that his lead has been attached. Hold the lead in your left hand and the treat in your right hand. Give him the treat but just allow him to lick it. Do not let him grab it. Now say the word "sit" and slowly

raise the treat to the ceiling. As your dog keeps looking at his treat will have to bend his knees and sit. When he sits give him a treat and praise him. Make sure that you praise him with a lot of enthusiasm. When a dog hears his owner praise him he feels extremely proud of his accomplishment.

b) Teaching your English Mastiff to stay down

When you know what your English Mastiff perceives when you give him the down command it becomes very easy for you to teach him to stay down. Usually for dogs the down position is a submissive state. When you start teaching your English Mastiff the down exercise try not to be too loud or overpowering will make him develop fear or will make him aggressive.

To train your dog to stay down keep him close to your leg and make him face the same direction as you. Now, hold a treat close to his nose and allow him to sniff it. In a very low tone, whisper the word "down" and keep the treat near his nose. Never allow him to grab the treat. Instead, just keep sliding it away from his nose and he will follow it. Place your left arm on the withers and urge him to move forward. Make sure your push is not too harsh. Gently press him down till he begins to inch towards the treat. As he inches forward, use, reinforcing sentences like," Good boy, I know you can do it" and keep sliding the treat away.

Lower the treat to the level of the floor and he will lower his head too. Now, slide the treat away from him while keeping it on the floor. When your English Mastiff sees the treat and hears your positive statements, he will feel motivated to go after the treat.

When he has come to the down position where he is resting on the elbows of the forearms, give him the treat. Make sure you praise him well before you hand over the treat to him. Try to keep your English Mastiff in the "down" position for as much time as possible. If you do not startle him or move too quickly, he is likely to stay in that position till you find something new for him to do. The idea is to keep your dog relaxed so that he doesn't feel threatened to let go of the "down" position and run.

c) Teaching your English Mastiff to Stay

Whether your English Mastiff is in a sitting position or in the down position, it is easy to tell him to maintain that particular position for a long time. This is again done with the help of praise and food. Simply giving your English Mastiff treats is not good enough. You must be able to clearly tell your English Mastiff what you expect from him.

While you may simply pat him and praise him when he is in the sitting or down position, it is a little different when you need him to stay. For this, you must step in front of your dog and place your toes in front of his. Now hold the treat in front of him in your right hand and say "stay" as you allow him to nibble and lick the treat. Do not release the treat for at least five seconds. After this, step to the side of the dog and release the treat immediately. This will teach your dog that holding himself in one particular position will get him a treat.

The next objective is to help him continue this behavior even when you are at a considerable distance from him. So, for the next few days, add a little distance between you and your English Mastiff before you give him the treat. As you are stepping away, face your palm towards your English Mastiff as a signal for him to stay. Show him the treat but do not allow him to smell or taste it. Eventually he will realize that as soon as you are back next to him, he will get that treat.

As your dog becomes familiar with the "stay" command, you can increase the distance and the time that you expect him to stay down for. After repeating this, you can be sure that your English Mastiff will stay until you go back to him or call him to you. Every time he displays a behavior that is correct, be generous in your praise.

You may also use a stop watch or a clock as a measure of the time that your English Mastiff is able to stay. This command is especially necessary when you are showing your English Mastiff.

If he is able to stay by himself for long periods of time and wait for your call, he is rewarded more obedience points.

Again, you must remember that your dog will stay only till he does not feel too threatened. The moment he hears a loud noise or sees sudden movement, his instinct will kick in. So, when you are teaching him commands such as stay and down, make sure that you take your English Mastiff to a quiet and secluded spot where there are no distractions that will get his mind away from the training objective.

d) Teaching your English Mastiff to come

The best way to teach your English Mastiff to come to you is to tell him that something fun is in order when he comes to you on command. Many owners try to threaten their dogs to come close to them. They may call the dog a couple of times and then use a rough "come" command if he does not obey. When you instill fear in your pet, it is a negative reinforcement. Just like Thorndike said, any activity that ends in a negative event is less likely to be repeated.

Instead, turn this into a game. One fun way to teach your English Mastiff to teach your English Mastiff to come to you is to tell every member of the family to hide in separate rooms with treats in their hand. Then call out to your dog and use commands like "Where are you? "Or "Come on, boy". Initially, your English Mastiff will not understand that there are treats waiting for him when he finds the members of your family.

However, he will instinctively try and look for you when he can hear your voice but cannot see you. So keep repeating the command till he actually finds you. When he does, greet him with very loud and obvious praises that he will get excited by. Of course, he will also find the treat waiting for him. As he discovers the rooms that each member of the family is in, let him be greeted in the same enthusiastic manner. This will teach him that the command "where are you" means celebration and fun.

If you have kids at home, this activity will become a lot more fun. As you know, kids simply love to play hide and seek. Now, they get to play this with their large, furry friend! The other advantage of using kids is that you can get them to hide in smaller places like the bath tub. So, your English Mastiff will have to work harder to find his treats and enjoy the celebration.

Once he gets used to it, all you need to do is enter a room and say "where are you" and your happy and enthusiastic English Mastiff will appear from nowhere to find you. This command is especially useful with lead dogs who need to get t their masters when called. Lead dogs are trained to help visually challenged people. When they are trained in this manner, there are very few instances or rather no instances when the dog is unable to find his master.

e) Teaching the English Mastiff to heel
We all have seen enthusiastic dogs that will never stop pulling on the lead when they are out on a walk. This is a habit that needs to be curbed at a very young age. You see, there are several things that may go wrong if you are unable to get your dog to walk beside you calmly without getting too excited. Remember that your English Mastiff is a really large dog. It will take just one strong pull for him to break the lead and run off. Sometimes, his pull might even be strong enough to dislocate your entire shoulder.

The command "heel" is meant to get your English Mastiff to walk beside you calmly when you take him out. Sometimes a distraction like a stray cat might get him excited and make him tug hard at the leash. Then, you must be able to get him to heel with a simple voice command.

To begin with, start by holding the loop end of the leash in your right hand. Take the English Mastiff close to your left leg and hold the leash closer to the collar with your left hand. With this, you have complete control over your English Mastiff. Walk three steps holding the leash this way so that your English Mastiff stays completely close to you. When you are done walking three steps, ask your English Mastiff to sit and praise him if he has walked without tugging. Try this again. If he continues to walk without tugging, you can increase the number of steps to five. Every time you start walking, give him the command so that he knows what he is responding to. Even after five steps if he is walking without tugging, allow him to sit and praise him. You must release the lead a little and give him a treat after you have praised him thoroughly. You may increase the number of steps each time you take your English Mastiff out for a heeling session. When you are done with the session, all you need to do is say "Ok" and release the tension on the leash. The word "Ok" is a release term whenever you are done with a training session for your English Mastiff.

If your dog is one that loves to tug and pull as you are walking, use the brake method. Grab the leash tightly and hold your ground. Do not move till your English Mastiff stops pulling and tugging. This is your way of establishing command and telling your English Mastiff that you will only go where it you want to go and that he is not appreciated for pulling on the lead.

After he has calmed down start walking. If he looks at you intently or slows his pace down and remains close to you, praise him and reward him well. In a few weeks, you will have a dog who is able to walk beside you politely without tugging and yanking too much.

The heeling session can be a little stressful on your Mastiff. So, after you have finished your session give him a chance to run around freely or just walk about without being held too close to you. This will help him relax and be calm.

5. Hand Signals

Hand signal training is by far the most useful and efficient training method for every dog. This is because all too often we inundate our canine companions with a great deal of chatter and noise that they really do not understand because English is not their first language. Contrary to what some humans might think, the first language of any dog, is a combination of sensing energy and watching body language, which requires no spoken word or sound. Therefore, when we humans take the time to teach our dog hand signals for all their basic commands, we are communicating with them at a level they instinctively understand, plus we are helping them to become a focused follower, as they must watch us to understand what is required of them.

If you teach your puppy hand signals from the beginning, it will be so much easier when your dog becomes a senior and his hearing is affected. That way, you can still easily communicate with your dog by using the hand signals he knows.

a) Hand signal to Come

Come: you can kneel down for this command or stay standing. Open your arms wide like you are hugging a very large tree. This hand signal can be seen from a long distance. When first teaching hand signals to your puppy, always show the hand signal for the command at the same time you say the word. If they are totally ignoring the command, it will be time to incorporate a lunge line, which is a very long leash to help you teach the "Come" command.

Simply attach a 20-foot line to their collar and let them sniff about in a large yard or at your neighborhood park. At your leisure, firmly ask them to "Come" and show the hand signal. If they do not immediately come to you, give a firm tug with the lunge line, so that they understand what you are asking of them.

If they still do not "Come" toward you, simply reel them in until they are in front of you. Then let them wander about again, until you are ready to ask them to "Come". Repeat this process until your puppy responds correctly at least 80% of the time. You can also reinforce the command by giving a treat when they come back to you when asked. Always ask them to "Sit" when they return to you.

b) Hand signal to Sit

Sit: right arm (palm open facing upward) parallel to the floor, and then raise your arm, while bent at the elbow toward your shoulder. Sit is a very simple, yet extremely valuable command for all puppies and dogs. If your dog is not sitting on command, try holding a treat above and slightly behind their head, so that when they look up for it they may automatically sit to see it.

Slowly remove the treats as reward and replace the treat with a "life reward", such as a chest rub or a scratch behind the ears and your happy smile. If your dog is not particularly treat motivated, lift up and slightly back on the leash when asking them to sit (stand in front of them), and if they still are having difficulties, reach down with your free hand, place it across your dog's back at the place where the back legs join the hip and gently squeeze.

Remember -- Do NOT simply push down on your dog's back to force their hind legs to collapse under them as this pressure could harm their spine or leg joints.

c) Hand signal to Stay

Stay: right armed fully extended toward your dog's head, palm open, hand bent up at the wrist. Once your dog is in the "Sit" position, ask them to "Stay" with both the verbal cue and the hand signal.

TIP: if you are right-handed, use your right arm and hand for the signal, and if you are left-handed, use your left arm and hand for the signal. Using your dominant hand will be much more effective because your strongest energy emanates from the palm of your dominant hand. While your dog is sitting and staying, slowly back away from them. If they move from their position, calmly put them back into Sit and ask them to "Stay" again, using both the verbal cue and the hand signal. Continue to practice this until your dog understands that you want them to stay sitting and not move toward you. With all commands, when your dog is just learning, be patient and always reward them with a treat and your happy praise for a job well done.

6. Simple Tricks

When teaching your dog tricks, in order to give them extra incentive, find a treat that they really like, and give the treat as rewards and to help solidify a good performance. Most dogs will be extra attentive during training sessions when they know that they will be rewarded with their favorite treats. If your puppy is less than six months old when you begin teaching them tricks, keep your training sessions short (no more than 5 or 10 minutes) and fun, and as they become adults, you can extend your sessions as they will be able to maintain their focus for longer periods of time.

a) Shake a Paw

Who doesn't love a dog that knows how to shake a paw? This is one of the easiest tricks to teach.

TIP: most dogs are naturally either right or left pawed. If you know which paw your dog favors, ask them to shake this paw.

Find a quiet place to practice, without noisy distractions or other pets, and stand or sit in front of your dog. Place them in the sitting position and have a treat in your left hand. Say the command *"Shake"* while putting your right hand behind their left or right paw and pulling the paw gently toward yourself until you are holding their paw in your hand. Immediately praise them and give them the treat. Most dogs will learn the "Shake" trick very quickly, and very soon, once you put out your hand, your dog will immediately lift their paw and put it into your hand, without your assistance or any verbal cue. Practice every day until they are 100% reliable with this trick, and then it will be time to add another trick to their repertoire.

b) Roll Over

You will find that just like your dog is naturally either right or left pawed, that they will also naturally want to roll either to the right or the left side. Take advantage of this by asking your dog to roll to the side they naturally prefer.

Sit with your dog on the floor and put them in a lie down position. Hold a treat in your hand and place it close to their nose without allowing them to grab it, and while they are in the lying position, move the treat to the right or left side of their head so that they have to roll over to get to it. You will very quickly see which side they want to naturally roll to, and once you see this, move the treat to this side. Once they roll over to this side, immediately give them the treat and praise them. You can say the verbal cue *"Over"* while you demonstrate the hand signal motion (moving your right hand in a circular motion) or moving the treat from one side of their head to the other with a half circle motion.

Roll Over: moving your right or left arm/hand in a small circular motion, in the direction you wish your dog to roll toward.

c) Sit Pretty

While this trick is a little more complicated, and most dogs pick up on it very quickly, remember that every dog is different so always exercise patience. Find a quiet space with few distractions and sit or stand in front of your dog and ask them to "Sit".

Have a treat nearby (on a countertop or table) and when they sit, use both of your hands to lift up their front paws into the sitting pretty position, while saying the command *"Sit Pretty"*. Help them balance in this position while you praise them and give them the treat. Once your dog can do the balancing part of the trick quite easily without your help, sit or stand in front of your dog while asking them to *"Sit Pretty"* and hold the treat above their head, at the level their nose would be when they sit pretty.

TIP: when first beginning this trick, place your dog beside a wall so they can use the wall to help them balance.

If they attempt to stand on their back legs to get the treat, you may be holding the treat too high, which will encourage them to stand on their back legs to reach it. Go back to the first step and put them back into the *"Sit"* position and again lift their paws while their backside remains on the floor.

Sit Pretty: hold your straight arm, fully extended, over your dog's head with a closed fist.   Make this a fun and entertaining time for your dog and practice a few times every day until they can *"Sit Pretty"* on hand signal command every time you ask.

A young puppy should be able to easily learn these basic tricks before they are six months old and when you are patient and make your training sessions short and fun for your dog, they will be eager to learn more

7. Overheating

Be very careful, when training or walking your dog outside during hot weather, so that you do not allow them to become overheated.

Always carry water with you to help keep them hydrated.

TIP: if your dog has a coat that is darker colored, you can easily help to keep them cooler on hot, sunny days by having them wear a light weight vest that is a lighter color than their own coat.

Remember that smaller dogs e.g. a puppy are close to heated pavement or road surfaces, which means that on a hot, sunny day, they will literally be heated from both the bottom and the top. If the pavement is very hot, do not allow them to walk on it. Instead, take them to a grassy area for their exercise.

8. Weaning the English Mastiff from his Food Reward

It is impossible to always carry treats around to give your English Mastiff. Also, you must make sure that he is able to respond solely to your calls and not just the treats. For this you must wean him off the treat that he is so used to.

Treats are great in the beginning when your dog is still unable to understand the command that you are giving him. He must be able to form the right association between a command and the acceptable behavior before you wean him off the treats. This process is gradual and you must never stop the rewards suddenly.

Usually, the dog receives a treat every time he performs a certain task correctly. When he is used to a certain voice command, reduce the number of treats that he gets. Give him his treats only at the end of every exercise sessions. When he is completely used to this new schedule, you can reduce the number of treats to every alternate exercise session. While you are weaning him, use a technique called the variable ratio reward system. This is when you mix a reward with praise. Sometimes you can give him both and sometimes you can hold back the treat. This will make your English Mastiff respond to the treat because he is still hopeful that a treat will come his way. Even if you do not give him a treat a couple of times, this hope will not be lost. However, verbal praise is a must as it is the real reinforcement for you English Mastiff. All he needs to know is that his master is proud of him for accomplishing certain goals.

9. The Need for Obedience Classes

Obedience classes are not mandatory. However, they work really well if you need to train your English Mastiff for showing. Of course, when you choose to have a English Mastiff mainly for showing purposes, you can also enroll in handling classes that will teach you how to handle your dog during the show.

There are several obedience classes that are available for you to enroll your English Mastiff into. It is best that you choose a class that is closest to your home to reduce the traveling stress that your English Mastiff might experience after a rigorous training session. If you are part of a dog club, you may enquire there for basic obedience classes. These clubs also offer classes that will prepare your English Mastiff for competitions. You may also hire local trainers who will come to your home and train your dog for you.

The type of obedience class that you choose depends upon your objective for training your English Mastiff. If you are just looking at having a well trained dog, all you need is to teach him the basic commands. If you are planning to enroll your English Mastiff in competitions, you must consider the level that he is competing at. In the initial levels, the basic commands are enough to earn him points. As your dog advances into various levels, you will have to put in more time and energy as these titles are highly acclaimed.

Usually, an obedience class for the earlier stages will last for about eight weeks. It is mandatory for the owner to accompany his English Mastiff. These sessions are generally about an hour long. You must also make time to make your English Mastiff practice the commands that he learns.

When you make it a point to follow the instructions provided at these classes, you will be able to take home a well mannered dog who takes interest in the activities that you like. The trainers who teach your dogs in these sessions are highly trained professionals who know what it takes to get the attention of various breeds of dogs. They understand the behavior and the temperament of your dog within minutes of introduction and will be able to create customized sessions that will bring out the best in your beloved canine buddy.

10. Surviving Adolescence

The adolescent period in a young dog's life, between the ages of 6 and 12 months, is the transitional stage of both physical and psychological development when they are physically almost full grown in size, yet their minds are still developing and they are testing their boundaries and the limits that their human counterparts will endure.

This can be a dangerous time in a puppy's life because this is when they start to make decisions on their own which, if they do not receive the leadership they need from their human guardians, can lead to developing unwanted behaviors. Learning how to make decisions on their own would be perfectly normal and desirable if your puppy was living in the wild, amongst a pack of dogs, because learning to make decisions would be necessary for their survival.

However, when living within a human environment, your puppy must always adhere to human rules and it will be up to their human guardians to continue their vigilant, watchful guidance in order to make sure that they do. Many humans are lulled into a false sense of security when their new puppy reaches the age of approximately six months, because the puppy has been well socialized, they have been to puppy classes and long since been house trained.

The real truth is that the serious work is only now beginning and the humans and their new puppy could be in for a time of testing that could seriously challenge the relationship and leave the humans wondering if they made the right decision to share their home with a dog. If the human side of the relationship is not prepared for this transitional time in their young dog's life, their patience may be seriously tried, and the relationship of trust and respect that has been previously built can be damaged, and could take considerable time to repair.

While not all adolescent puppies will experience a noticeable adolescent period of craziness, because every puppy is different, most young dogs do commonly exhibit at least some of the usual adolescent behaviors, including reverting to previous puppy behaviors. Some of these adolescent behaviors might include destructive chewing of objects they have previously shown no interest in, selective hearing or ignoring previously learned commands, displaying aggressive behavior, jumping on everyone, barking at everything that moves, or reverting to relieving themselves in the house, even though they were house trained months ago.

Keeping your cool and recognizing these adolescent signs is the first step toward helping to make this transition period easier on your puppy and all family members.

The first step to take that can help keep raging hormones at bay, is to spay or neuter your puppy just prior to the onset of adolescence, at around four or five months of age. While spaying or neutering a puppy will not entirely eliminate the adolescent phase, it will certainly help and at the same time will spare your puppy the added strain of both the physical and emotional changes that occur during sexual maturity.

As well, some female puppies will become extremely aggressive toward other dogs during a heat, and non-neutered males may become territorially aggressive and pick fights with other males. Once your puppy has been spayed or neutered, you will want to become more active with your young dog, both mentally and physically by providing them with continued and more complex disciplined exercises.

This can be accomplished by enrolling your adolescent in a dog whispering session or more advanced training class, which will help them to continue their socialization skills while also developing their brain. Even though it may be more difficult to train during this period, having the assistance of a professional and continuing the experience of ongoing socialization amongst other dogs of a similar size can be invaluable, as this is the time when many young dogs begin to show signs of antisocial behavior with other dogs as well as unknown humans.

When your dog is provided with sufficient daily exercise and continued socialization with unfamiliar dogs, people and places that provides interest and expands their mind, they will be able to transition through the adolescent stage of their life much more seamlessly.

11. The Unruly Adolescent

If your puppy happens to be especially unruly during their adolescent phase, you will need to simply limit their opportunities for making mistakes. For instance, a puppy who is digging up the yard, or chewing up just about anything they can get their teeth on will need to be closely supervised so that you can direct their energy into less harmful pursuits.

It does absolutely no good to yell at your puppy for engaging in behavior you are not happy with, and in fact, yelling or getting angry will only desensitize your young dog from listening to any of your commands. Further, although you may eventually get the results you want, if you yell loud enough, your puppy will then be reacting out of fear, rather than respect, and this will be damaging to your relationship. Displaying calm, yet assertive energy is the ONLY energy that works well to help your adolescent puppy understand what is required of them.

All other human emotions (frustration, anger, impatience, sadness, excitement) are "read" by puppies and dogs as being unstable, and not only will the smart and sensitive dog not understand these emotions, they will not respect you for displaying these types of unstable energies. An extremely rambunctious adolescent dog may need to have their free run of the house curtailed so that they are confined to areas where you can easily supervise them.

Make sure they are within eyesight at all times, so that if they do find an opportunity to make a mistake, you can quickly show them what is permitted and what is not.

Adolescence may also be a time when you might have to insist that your young dog sleeps in their crate with the door closed whenever you cannot supervise, as well as at bedtime so they continue to understand that you have firm rules. As well, keeping on top of house training is also a good idea during the adolescent period of your puppy's life because some adolescent puppies may become stubborn and forget that they are already house trained.

This means actually taking the time to be involved in the process by leashing up your dog and physically taking them outside whenever they need to relieve themselves. This sort of a routine is also a disciplined exercise that will help to reinforce in your puppy's mind, that you are the boss. Too many humans with convenient yards simply do not participate at all in the bathroom routine of their young dogs and thereby miss out on endless opportunities to reinforce who is the boss.

12. Rewarding Unwanted Behavior

Often humans make the mistake of accidentally rewarding unwanted behaviors. It is very important to recognize that any attention paid to an overly excited, out of control, adolescent puppy, even negative attention, is likely going to be rewarding for your puppy. Therefore, when you engage with an out of control puppy, you end up actually rewarding them, which will encourage them to continue more of this unwanted behavior.

Be aware that chasing after a puppy when they have taken something they are not supposed to have, picking them up when they are barking or showing aggression, pushing them off when they jump on you or other people, or yelling when they refuse to come when called, are all forms of attention that can actually be rewarding for most puppies.

As your dog's guardian, it will be your responsibility to provide calm and consistent structure for your puppy, which will include finding acceptable and safe ways to allow your puppy to vent their energy without being destructive or harmful to property, other dogs, humans, or the actual puppy. Activities that create or encourage an overly excited puppy, such as rough games of tug-o-war, or wild games of chase through the living room, should be immediately curtailed, so that your adolescent puppy learns how to control their energy and play quietly and appropriately without jumping on everyone or engaging in barking or mouthy behavior. Further, if your adolescent puppy displays excited energy simply from being petted by yourself, your family members or any visitors, you will need to teach yourself, your family and your friends to ignore your puppy until they calm down. Otherwise, you will be teaching your puppy that the touch of humans mean excitement. For instance, when you continue to engage with an overly excited puppy, you are rewarding them for out of control behavior and literally teaching them that when they see humans, you want them to display excited energy.

Worse, once your puppy has learned that humans are a source of excitement, you will then have to work very long and hard to reverse this behavior.

Children are often a source of excitement that can cause an adolescent puppy to be extremely wound up. Do not allow your children to engage with an adolescent puppy unless you are there to supervise and teach the children appropriate and calm ways to interact with the puppy.
In order to keep everyone safe, it is very important that your puppy learns at an early age that neither children nor adults are sources of excitement.

You can help develop the mind of an adolescent dog and the minds of growing children at the same time by teaching children that your puppy needs structured walks and by showing them how to play fetch, search, hide and seek, or how to teach the puppy

157

simple tricks and obedience skills that will be fun and positive interaction for everyone.

13. Giving Up is Not an Option

Too often we humans get frustrated and give up on our dogs when they change from being the cute, cuddly and mostly obedient little puppy they once were, and become all kinds of trouble you never bargained for, as they grow into their adolescent stage. Often times, it will be during the confusing adolescent stage of a dog's life that they find themselves abandoned and behind bars as their humans who promised to love and protect them, leave their once loved fur friend at the local pound or SPCA.

First of all, not all dogs go through a crazy adolescent period, and secondly, even if they do, please read this section carefully humans, because you can live through puppy adolescence and come out the other side relatively unscathed and a much more knowledgeable and patient guardian. Congratulations are in order if you've been successful with potty training your young puppy and with teaching them to sleep in their own kennel at night. As well, you've taught your puppy their first few basic commands, and socialized them with many other dogs, people and places, so you should feel proud of all your accomplishments and the leaps and bounds you and your puppy have accomplished together over the last several months.

Even though your adolescent puppy may be starting to act like a Tasmanian devil, and you may be having second thoughts, now is not the time to give up on them and yourself just because it may seem like someone switched your dog when you weren't looking.

Now is the time to remain calmly consistent and persistent, and to know that you will eventually be able to enjoy the happy rewards of your entire puppy raising diligence. Yes, it can be quite a shock when what used to be your well behaved little darling who never chewed anything they weren't supposed to suddenly takes it into their head eat all the tassels off your Persian rug or chew through a seat belt in your vehicle during the short 15 minutes you were shopping. Even more disconcerting might be when your previously obedient and loving puppy, who always listened to your directions, suddenly appears to have gone deaf and can't remember their name when you call them to follow you inside the house, and instead they take off running after a cat three blocks away. And then, what happened to that quiet little puppy that never appeared to have a mean bone in their body that now spends most of their time at the window barking and growling at everything and everyone passing by?

Welcome to the world of canine adolescence where it appears that your puppy has turned into some sort of monster and all your previous hard work was for naught. Of course, this dramatic switch from being the world's best puppy into the monster you can no longer control is not true for all puppies, as every puppy is unique. However, being prepared for the worst will help you ride any impending storm and get you both out the other side where you can enjoy an even closer relationship than you previously had. If you are at the stage with your puppy that you are having great difficulties and wondering if you made the right decision to share your home with a dog, rest assured that puppy adolescence is a normal phase of their development, which can be managed, and which will definitely pass. As well, if you are finding yourself totally overwhelmed, there are many professionals who can provide valuable assistance to help you through this stage of your puppy's development.

For most puppies, adolescence will begin between the ages of five and seven months and this is also the time that you need to be making an appointment at your veterinarian's office to have your puppy spayed or neutered. Although neutering or spaying will not prevent adolescent behavior entirely, it can certainly reduce the intensity of it, as during this period there are hormonal changes occurring that will affect your puppy's behavior.

While it's usually hormones that are the major cause of behavioral changes in your adolescent puppy, there are also physical changes occurring at the same time that you may not be aware of. For instance, your puppy will be going through physical growth spurts which might be causing them some pain, as well as changes related to growth in their brain while your puppy's cerebral cortex becomes more involved in thinking for itself. Usually, during this time of brain growth, a puppy will be trying to make choices for themself, and may or may not yet be capable of making the right choices. This is why their behavior can appear to be quite erratic.

During the early adolescent period of brain development in your puppy, the signals sometimes get mixed up and rerouted, which can result in the perplexing responses you might notice, when for instance, you ask you puppy to sit and they stare dumbly at you, even though they learned this command months ago.

Don't worry because your previous training will return.

14. Other Activities for your English Mastiff

When your English Mastiff has been trained to follow the basic commands mentioned above, you will be able to enjoy quality time with him. A well trained English Mastiff knows how to behave himself. So, you can easily include him in several other activities in your life without the fear of him disrupting the flow, causing any damage or injuring himself and others around him.

Once you have mastered the basic control tactics, it becomes very easy for you to handle your English Mastiff. Remember that during these training sessions, you have also learnt about the body language of your dog and even he has gained a lot of knowledge about your moods and expectations. This understanding makes it much easier for the two of you to communicate with one another.

Now, you can teach your dog things like helping around the house and even taking care of small responsibilities around your farm or yard. When your English Mastiff learns to hand out with you, your life becomes much easier. You need not constantly worry about leaving the English Mastiff alone at home or making arrangements for him while you are away. Instead, you can simply take him along. You will see that your English Mastiff makes a great, reliable companion.

One of the best activities that you can indulge in with your English Mastiff is hiking or trekking. He can perform this activity with little or no help from your side. He will need to know simple commands like "heel" "sit" and "stay" for you to be sure that he is safe during each trekking expedition. Your English Mastiff will love this activity as it is great exercise that includes his favorite activities like walking and running.

15. Make Sure He Gets Enough Exercise

Exercise is the most important thing for a English Mastiff. Just as exercise is important for you, it is necessary for your English Mastiff as well. Here are some benefits of exercising:

• For proper skeletal and muscular development, your English Mastiff must be exercised on a regular basis.
• For proper metabolism of the food that you give your English Mastiff, getting him proper exercise is mandatory.

• Your English Mastiff requires ample space in the outdoors to sprawl and get enough fresh air to grow well.

• A English Mastiff will be able to keep himself mentally stimulated and active when he is allowed to run and play outside.

• The chances of your dog becoming aggressive will be reduced to a large extent. Since the negative energy gets redirected with exercise, your English Mastiff will be less destructive or aggressive.

- Playing with your English Mastiff is the best way to bond with him. Of course, you can save on expensive gym memberships!

The best exercise for a English Mastiff is a good long walk. As you have already read in the earlier chapters, your English Mastiff is not exactly an active dog. So you do not have to be too athletic to give your English Mastiff the right exercise that is required for your English Mastiff. You can also plan playing sessions with your English Mastiff in your yard. He will love to fetch, but don't expect too much speed from him. He has a humongous body!

A dog as large as the English Mastiff should never be over exercised. You must always increase the pace of the exercise for your English Mastiff for his own safety. You can start with short walks and increase the length of the walks and the speed of the walks as you continue. You must also never push him too hard to perform tricks, fetch or play with you.

16. Electronic Training Devices

Generally speaking, positive training methods are far more effective than using devices that involve negative stimulation.

Further, unless you are training a dog to hunt badgers or rabbits, using electronic devices is usually a excuse for a lazy human who will not take the time to properly train their dog by teaching them rules and boundaries which leads to respect and an attentive follower. When you do not provide your dog with a consistent leadership role that teaches your dog to trust, respect and listen to you in all circumstances, you will inevitably experience behavioral issues.

Electronic training devices such as e-collars, spray collars or electronic fencing all rely upon negative, painful or stressful reinforcement, which can easily cause a sensitive dog to become nervous or live a life of fear. For instance, a dog simply cannot understand the principles of "invisible" boundaries, and therefore, should never be subjected to the confusion of the punishment that occurs when walking across an invisible line within their own home territory.

Dogs naturally understand the positive training methods of receiving a reward, which is not only much more efficient and effective when teaching boundaries, rewards are far kinder, and create a much stronger bond with your dog.

The Truth About Shock Collars

First of all, it would have to be an extremely rare situation in which it would be necessary or recommended that you use a shock collar as these devices are usually only employed in extreme situations. However, for large breeds who could seriously harm someone, sometimes these devices are used.

The use of remote, electronic, shock or *"e-collars"* is at best a controversial subject that can quickly escalate into heated arguments.

In certain, rare circumstances, and when used correctly, the e-collar can be a helpful training tool that could actually save a dog's life if they are acting out in dangerous ways.

An e-collar would generally be utilized in a circumstance where a larger breed of dog has access to free range over a large property, resulting in difficulties getting their attention from a distance if they become distracted by other animals or smells.

Many dogs that have not been properly trained from a young age also learn that when they are off leash and out of your immediate reach that they can choose to ignore your commands, bark their heads off, terrorize the neighbors or chase wildlife. Generally e-collars can be effective training tools for working breed herding or hunting or tracking dogs.

Chapter 12: Training Your English Mastiff

In these types of circumstances a remote training collar can be an effective training device for reinforcing verbal commands from a great distance, such as "Come", "Sit" or "Stay". Finally, electronic collars can be used as a last resort to help teach a dog not to engage in a dangerous behavior that could result in them being seriously harmed or even killed.

Electronic Fencing

Honestly, there are far more reasons NOT to install an electronic fence as a means of keeping your dog inside your yard, than there are good reasons for considering one. For instance, a dog whose yard is surrounded by an electronic fence can quite easily develop fear, aggression, or both, directed toward what they may believe is the cause of the shock they are receiving.

As a result, installing an electronic fence may cause your dog to become aggressive toward cats, other dogs, other humans, other wildlife, children riding by on bikes or skateboards, the mail carrier, or the dog next door.

As well, a dog that receives a fright, or in excitement forgets about the shock they are going to receive, may run through an electronic fence and then be too frightened or stressed to come back home because it means that they must pass through the painful barrier again. Further, it is actually possible that electronic fencing may encourage a dog to escape the yard simply because they associate their yard with pain. This feeling can be reinforced if a dog escapes the electronic yard and then is again punished by the shock when they attempt to come home. Another factor to keep in mind with respect to electronic fencing is that other dogs or teasing children can freely enter the yard and torment or attack your dog, and a thief bent on stealing your dog will be able to do so with ease.

The absolute best way to keep your dog safe in their own yard, while helping to establish your role as guardian and leader, is to be out there with them while they are on leash, and to only permit them freedom in your yard under your close supervision.

Chapter 13: Travelling with your English Mastiff

1) Travelling

Your English Mastiff cannot be confined to home all the time. There are times when it becomes very necessary to travel. For instance the various trips that have to be made to the vet. There could be times when you have to go out of town and your English Mastiff cannot be left back at home. So if he is not prepared for this travel your English Mastiff may feel out of place in a moving vehicle. The travel could be either by car, rail or flight. There are a few tips for preparing your English Mastiff to travel by the various modes of transport.

Travel by car

The English Mastiff must be prepared to travel by car at a very early age. Although the trips by car may not be frequent, there may be instances once in a while when you have to visit the vet. This is when you need to take your English Mastiff by car. If he is not used to riding in a car the whole drive could be traumatic for the English Mastiff. In order to make the ride less traumatic and less troublesome you need to take certain precautions.

If your English Mastiff is used to a crate at home then the same crate may be used to travel in the car. If it is an adult English Mastiff then a bigger vehicle would be required to accommodate your English Mastiff. Initially you can try placing your puppy in a crate while travelling in the car. In case you feel he is not comfortable then he can be placed on the lap of another person while you are driving. This arrangement would be perfect till

166

your English Mastiff is just a puppy. But you need to make alternate arrangements when he grows up to be an adult.

There are safety harnesses specially designed for dogs which are much like a seat belt which would strap your English Mastiff to the seat. This would shield your English Mastiff from getting injured or thrown out when there is a sudden jerk. Never let the English Mastiff loose in the vehicle. He may climb over you and pester you which would be quite distracting whistle driving and this is very unsafe for you as well as your English Mastiff.

If you have planned a long trip then make sure you carry along some paper towels and some old bath towels. You might have to stop to let the dog relieve himself. This should be followed by cleaning him up and for this you will require the paper towels. If your English Mastiff were to suffer from motion sickness you may need old bath towels to clean him up. In case the weather is warm then you need to carry water with you to feed your English Mastiff.

When the car is parked make sure not to leave your English Mastiff alone since the heat inside the car could be very overpowering when the windows are up. Cars tend to get heated up very soon even when parked in shade when the windows are up. If the windows are kept open, there is always a chance that your English Mastiff would hurt himself while trying to get out of the car.

While going on a long trip make sure that the hotels on the way are dog friendly since many of the hotels do not allow dogs. Carrying ice with you will be a very good idea if you are travelling in warm weather since you may need it when your English Mastiff gets overheated.

Travel by air

There are certain specifications to be followed while travelling with your dog by air. For this you need to make enquiries with the airlines you choose to travel by. There are specifications

167

regarding the size, type and labeling of the crate. To make him feel more comfortable you should add his favorite toy in his crate. Your English Mastiff should not be fed hours before the travel to make sure that his need to relieve himself minimizes.

If you are planning a long trip attaching food and water bowels to the crate is recommended so the airline authorities will be able to feed him in between the trip.

The most important aspect is identification of your pet since you will be travelling in separate sections. There should be an ID tag attached to his crate with your contact information. This would eliminate the risk of getting separated from your dog.

While planning a long trip the most important item in the agenda will be accommodation. Make sure that the place of your stay is dog-friendly. If you end making stay arrangements without ensuring whether the hotel is dog-friendly then you may end up without a place to stay if it is against their rules to allow a dog to stay.

Travel abroad

If you plan to travel abroad and choose not to take your English Mastiff along, then you will have to make alternate arrangements for him while you are away. The following would be your options:

- Have him to stay with your neighbor while you are away
- Request your friend either to stay at your place or visit your place frequently to monitor and feed your English Mastiff
- Put him in a kennel. If you plan to keep your English Mastiff in a kennel while you are away, you should make sure well advance that the kennel is clean and hygienic. Also make sure that there is sufficient place for your dog to play and exercise. But before boarding him in a kennel make enquiries about the kennel from various sources. Enquire as to how they treat the pets. Whether they spend sufficient time with the pets and whether they play with them etc. Your English Mastiff is

your priced possession. He is your friend and your companion. You need to take extra care as to where you are boarding him while you are away. If you are boarding him in a place like a kennel where he comes in contact with other dogs you need to be extra cautious. So you need to make special enquiries about the vaccination policy of the kennel. This is very necessary especially when it concerns the safety of your dog since he comes in contact with other dogs and chances of acquiring infectious diseases are very high.

Identification of your dog

Your English Mastiff is your priced possession and your best friend. You would never want him to be out of your sight and the thought of losing him will make you shudder. So let us imagine what would happen if he were to wriggle out of his collar and run away from you. First of all make sure that this never happens. That he would never wriggle out of his collar and let himself loose. But eventualities do happen. Your dog might run away from you.

Under such circumstances how would you find your dog? Proper identification would enable the finder of your dog to return him to you safely. The following are the various options for proper identification of your dog.

a) A simple tag with contact details
These are the simple metal or plastic plaques that you put around your dog's collar. Your dog should were this collar at all times.

b) Micro-Chipping
A microchip implant is a tiny integrated circuit, approximately twice the size of a large grain of rice, enclosed in glass that is implanted under the skin of a dog (or other animal) with a syringe. The chip uses passive Radio Frequency Identification (RFID) technology, and is also known as a PIT tag (Passive Integrated Transponder).

The microchip is usually implanted, without anesthetic, into the scruff of a dog's neck by a veterinarian or shelter. The microchip has no internal power source, which means that they must be read by a scanner or *"interrogator"* which energizes the capacitor in the chip, which then sends radio signals back to the scanner so that the identifying number can be read.

Manufacturers of microchips often donate scanners to animal shelters and veterinarian clinics and hospitals. While many communities are proposing making micro-chipping of all dogs mandatory, such as N. Ireland, and micro-chipping is a requirements for any dogs traveling to the state of Hawaii, many others are not especially pleased with this idea because they believe it's just more big business for little reward.

For instance, while approximately one quarter of European dogs have a microchip implant, the idea is definitely lacking in popularity in the United States, where only 5% of dogs are micro-chipped. Even though micro-chipping is used by animal shelters, pounds, animal control officers, breeders and veterinarians, in order to help return a higher percentage of lost canines to their owners, some of the resistance to this idea can be explained by inherent problems with the ability of some organizations to correctly read the implants.

As an example, if the scanner is not tuned to the same frequency as the implanted microchip, it will not be read, which renders the process useless. Pet microchips are manufactured with different frequencies, including 125 kHz, 128 kHz and 134.2 kHz. While approximately 98% of the pet microchips in the US use 125 kHz, those in Europe use 134.2 kHz.

In other words, if the facility reading your dog's microchip does not have a compatible scanner, your dog will not be identified and returned to you. Further, what may turn out to be worse than the scanner incompatibility problem could be increasing evidence to indicate that microchips might cause cancer.

As well some microchips will migrate inside the dog's body and while they may start out in the dogs neck, they could end up in their leg or some other body part. You will have to weigh information known about microchips, including possible cancer risks, and the odds of losing your dog against whether or not a microchip is something you want to have for your dog.

Whether or not you choose a microchip for your dog, generally the cost ranges between $25 and $50 (£15 and £30) depending on what your veterinarian may charge for this service.

c) Tattooing

Dogs are tattooed to help identify them in case they are lost or stolen and many dog guardians prefer this safe, simple solution over micro-chipping. Tattooing does not require locating a scanner that reads the correct frequency and there are no known side effects. The tattoo can be the telephone number of the owner or the name of the owner . Because a tattoo is visible, it is immediately recognizable and reported when a lost dog is found, which means that tattooing could easily be the most effective means of identification available. As well, dog thieves are less likely to steal a dog that has a permanent visible form of identification. There are several registries for tattooed dogs, including the National Dog Tattoo Registry in the UK, which has a network of Accredited Tattooists across the UK.

The fee for tattooing and registering a dog for their lifetime is approximately £25. In the United States, the National Dog Registry (NDR) was founded in 1966 and since then, NDR has supervised, directed, conducted, or overseen the tattooing of more than 6 million animals. The cost for tattooing a single dog is approximately $10. plus a one-time registration fee of $45.

Local veterinary clinics do both micro chipping and tattooing. You can contact your veterinarian and breeder for the services. Some vets offer these services at their premises for a very nominal fee. After this make sure to register your dog with a legitimate national data base.

2) Finding Your Lost Dog

If your dog goes missing, there are many places you can contact and steps you can take that may help you locate your lost dog, including:

• Retracing your dog's last known location;

• Contacting your friends and neighbors;

• Putting up flyers on telephone poles throughout your neighborhood, with your contact details and a photograph of your dog;

• Calling all local shelters and pounds every day;

• Contacting local rescue organizations;

• Contacting your breeder;

• Contacting local schools -- children might have seen your dog in their neighborhood;

• Distributing flyers with a photograph of your dog and your contact details in all neighborhood stores and businesses;

• Contacting all businesses that deal with lost pets;

• Posting a picture on your Facebook or other social media;

• Asking your local radio station for help;

• Advertising in your local newspaper.

Chapter 14: The Health of Your English Mastiff

With breeds like the English Mastiff, there are several health problems that have been inherited from ancestors. There are also some diseases like cancer that are common to both people and animals. For most of these diseases, we are well aware of the condition when it comes to human beings. However, there are cases when these diseases might be similar in their symptoms but are extremely different in the cure and their manifestation in the canines. So, treatments vary drastically. The point I am trying to make here is that many owners don't consider their dogs as physiologically different. So, if the dog has a fever, they would probably mix the medicine that they would normally take in that situation. This practice is wrong as you must, as a rule, take your dog to a vet when he is unwell.

The first step to healthcare for an English Mastiff is finding a good vet. Since your English Mastiff is a special breed, the doctor who will treat him will also need to have special qualifications.

1. Selecting a Vet for Your English Mastiff

Usually, pet owners select doctors who have the right personality to take care of a breed as large as the English Mastiff. While this is a very important quality, the more important thing is that your vet must be easily accessible. In case of an emergency, your vet must be available immediately. The ride to your vet must not take more than 10 to 15 minutes.

The next thing that you will check for is the services that your vet offers. Now some of you may have specialized needs like tattooing or even grooming for your English Mastiff. You may also require a vet who is able to provide you with the most sophisticated and advanced pet care products. Of course, these services must be timely and must be able to reach you when you want. The responsiveness of your vet and his team to your requests is a very important factor in choosing a certain clinic.

Usually a vet will have all his degrees and certificates on display in his waiting room. While these certificates give you a basic knowledge of the education that your vet has had, there might be some specialized services that your vet may have to provide for your English Mastiff. This will require internships or specialized degrees that will equip your doctor to deal with specific problems. For instance, a veterinary cardiologist will specialize in understanding the functions of your Mastiffs heart better than any average vet.

You will need specialized attention for your dog when his condition is critical. Now, most veterinarians will perform routine checkups and even simple surgeries. However, you must look for a vet with more experience and knowledge when the condition that you are addressing is severe.

The next thing that is of great concern is the cost of your vet. If he is too expensive in comparison to other vets in your locality, you may want to look further. Never be shy to discuss costs with your vet. Ultimately, any decision that you take with respect to your dogs care is also bound by certain financial restrictions.

After you have taken all these things into consideration, you can take your puppy for the first visit. This is when you have an opportunity to scrutinize the staff and also the doctor who is dealing with your dog. If you are content with the services that you get, you may continue.

Remember, the vet that you choose for your English Mastiff must be the one who takes care of your dog on a regular basis. So, when you choose, choose wisely. Your vet will also become your reliable companion as your dog grows up. So, being able to relate to him and getting along with him also matter when you give the final nod.

2. Preventive Healthcare for an English Mastiff

When you go to a breeder to buy a puppy, he will only choose ones that are born from a dam whose disease profile is well known. Most breeders will give you a health certificate to tell you what problems you must look out for in your English Mastiff. Just to be sure, you can also visit the vet who treated the dam of your English Mastiff puppy to understand the problems that your puppy might have inherited. While the dam may pass on the ability to resist certain diseases, she may also pass on parasites and infections to your puppy. As the first step of preventive health care, you must learn everything possible about the health of the dam.

The next step is to get your English Mastiff vaccinated and thus, immunize him from the most probable diseases. There is a schedule that you must follow for these vaccinations for them to be most effective for your English Mastiff.

Vaccination schedule for your English Mastiff

The best thing to do when you bring your English Mastiff home is to have him tested thoroughly by a vet. It is a great idea to start a vaccination program when your puppy is still very young. In the first examination, the general health, the skeletal structure and the teeth of the English Mastiff are examined thoroughly. After this, you must fix up regular vaccination schedules that will help maintain the health of your English Mastiff.

Most of the vaccinations given to dogs are administered in the form of injections. They must be given only by a vet. It is recommended that you and your vet keep a record of each vaccination to ensure that a schedule is maintained. Most breeders will recommend that you give your English Mastiff his first vaccination only after 10 weeks. Usually, the dam passes on antibodies that last for at least 8 weeks. So starting the vaccination schedule after this will help maintain the effect of the naturally passed on anti bodies.

Most often, vaccinations are scheduled at intervals of 15 days or on a 15 day cycle. You must always take the advice provided by your vet as the dosage and the cycle will depend upon the type of vaccination that is being administered to your dog.

The vaccinations provided to puppies are usually meant for viruses. The usually vaccinations provided are for hepatitis, parainfluenza, distemper and parvovirus. Most of these vaccinations that you provide your puppy with will require a booster shot after he is a year old and also once after that. Once you have fixed the schedule with your vet, make sure you stick to it and keep it regular.

3. Common Health Problems with an English Mastiff

There are some diseases that are common to the English Mastiff. While some of these diseases affect most dog breeds, others are specific to the English Mastiff and are acquired through their genes.

Hip Dysplasia

This is a problem that is quite common in large dogs such as the English Mastiff. This is a problem of the ball and socket joint of the hip. There are several genetic and environmental factors that have been held responsible for the development of this condition. Research also shows that there is a very complex inheritance pattern for this disorder. There are multiple genes that are responsible for this condition.

This is the most common skeletal problem that has been observed in dogs, especially the large ones like your English Mastiff. When a dog has hip dysplasia, his joints are not fully developed. As the dog grows older, the joint deteriorates until the hip joint becomes incapable of functioning.

This condition normally begins when the English Mastiff is about four months old. Sometimes the onset of this disease is a little later when the dog develops skeletal issues like osteoarthritis. In this condition, joint inflammations begin to form. These inflammations lead to serious deterioration and disintegration of the joints.

Symptoms:

The symptoms that are observed in a dog with hip dysplasia depend on several conditions like the amount of laxity in the joints, the degree of inflammation of the joints and the duration of the condition in the animal. The most common symptoms include:

- Looseness or laxity in the joints
- Degeneration of the joints.
- Reduced Activity
- Inability and Hesitation while rising
- Hesitation while jumping or using the stairs
- Lameness in the hind limb
- Gait that is swaying
- Keeping the hind legs unnaturally close while standing
- Evident discomfort around the hip joint
- Joint movement accompanied by grating
- Reduced range of motion in the hips
- Reduction in the mass around the quads
- Enlargement of the muscles around the shoulder due to excessive load on the shoulders.

Causes
- Genetic Inheritance
- Obesity
- Lack of Nutrition
- Too much mass in the pelvic region

Diagnosis

Your vet might insist on getting a blood profile of your English Mastiff to check for any reduction in the blood count. Since inflammation and joint laxity are important factors in determining the severity of the condition, some physical examinations may also be necessary. X rays are useful in studying the extent of damage caused by the condition. Your doctor may also want to study the parentage of your English Mastiff to understand the potential danger of the condition to the functionality and well being of your English Mastiff. For this you may have to arrange for an interaction between your breeder and the Vet.

Treatment

Usually, English Mastiffs who have hip dysplasia are treated on an outpatient basis. Surgery is recommended only in severe cases. In the initial stages, exercises like swimming are very useful in controlling the condition. Watching the weight and diet of your English Mastiff is also important in controlling the amount of damage possible.

Skin problems in the English Mastiff

There are several skin problems that affect Mastiffs. It is a fact that vets are consulted for skin problems in dogs more than any other recorded condition. Even if you see that the dog is displaying visual symptoms similar to humans, you must never assume that it is the same disorder. They may also be many skin creams that are available at pet stores. These creams are only useful when it comes to treating the symptoms. If you want to treat the underlying problem, consult a vet. The common skin problems in Mastiffs are:

Hereditary skin problems

Sometimes, both the parents of the English Mastiff might seem completely normal. However, one or both may carry a recessive gene for a particular skin disorder. If this recessive gene is expressed in the English Mastiff, he will display the condition. The most common hereditary skin problems are cuta English Mastiffus asthenia, sebaceous adenitis, dermatomytisis and nodular dermatofibrosis. Most of these skin disorders may also have secondary diseases like cancer and respiratory diseases associated with them. Therefore, it is mandatory to have these conditions checked by veterinarians.

Parasite Bites

When a dog is bitten by a parasite, he may just scratch or bite the area. He will respond to a parasite only when he has been bitten. Most of these parasite bites lead to inflammation of the skin, eruptions and also infections. The sad thing is that before your English Mastiff has reached out and scratched the parasite, the damage is already done. Sometimes, the parasite may also have laid eggs that may aggravate the problems in the future. When parasites bite into the skin of the English Mastiff, they also leave behind the saliva which causes itching and irritation.

Auto Immune Skin Problems

These problems occur when the body begins to fight against itself. The most common auto immune skin problems include lupus that is common to dogs and humans. Of course, the symptoms are different for people and canines. These auto immune diseases, if not treated correctly, can lead to the death of Your English Mastiff. It is not transmissible. These conditions are usually treated with corticosteroids quite effectively.

Acral Lick Dermatitis

This is a condition that affects several breeds of dogs. However, it is quite poorly understood. This condition occurs when a dog licks a particular part of his body again and again. The lick is so intense sometimes that the hair from that region is removed. Since this condition is not known fully, the cure is not known either. It may be controlled to a certain extent using corticosteroids.

179

Allergies

Just like people, dogs are also prone to air borne allergies. The reaction of the dog when he has an allergen such as pollen on his body is similar to the presence of a parasite. He will bite and scratch that area rigorously. In the process, he may damage the area or cause wounds that are deep and painful.

Food problems in the English Mastiff

There are several diseases that are food related. While some of them might be internal, the others might have external causal factors like allergens and toxins that make their way into the dog's stomach through processed artificial foods that are easily available on stands.

Allergies

There are several foods that dogs are allergic to. You must keep a close watch on your pet when you introduce him to any food group or brand. Sometimes, even the most popular and highly recommended may not work well with your English Mastiff. It is best to consult your vet if you notice that the problem persists. He may be able to identify a certain element that your dog is allergic to. Replacing the food brand that you currently use with a brand that replaces the allergen can yield positive results.

Intolerance

When your English Mastiff is unable to digest certain foods, he is said to be intolerant to that particular food. For instance, many dogs may not be able to digest cow's milk. The most common symptoms of food intolerance are stomach pain, passing gas and also eliminating loose bowels.

Usually, it is quite hard to diagnose these issues as the symptoms are very few. With the help of your vet, however, you should be able to find the reason for your English Mastiff's discomfort. If the problem is an allergy or intolerance, the best way to deal with it is to put your English Mastiff on a diet that is recommended by your vet. You can also eliminate elements and food groups that are causing problems. In case of infections and internal issues, your vet will also administer oral medication.

Parasites:

There are two types of parasites that dogs have to deal with: Internal Parasites and External Parasites. Some of these parasites form a symbiotic relationship with the dog and actually promote good health. The problem arises when the parasites that are found on or inside the body of the parasite results in painful symptoms that do not allow a dog to function normally.

Ectoparasites

The parasites that live on the body of the English Mastiff are known as ecto parasites. The most common ectoparasites are:

• Fleas: Every dog owner is familiar with the dreadful problem of fleas. The problem with fleas is that they often multiply at an uncontrollable rate. They also lay eggs that will cause the problem to become prolonged. Fleas are usually a problem during the summer months. As soon as a flea hatches, it needs a host to feed on. Once it has found a host, it will never leave voluntarily. These fleas suck the blood of the host, leaving his skin irritable and itchy. You can control the problem of fleas by using creams and powders to eliminate them after they have grown into adults and to eliminate them in the pre adult stage. You will also have to clean the sofas, carpets and other possible hiding spots for fleas as well.

• Ticks: they are usually found in tropical and temperate areas. The treatment is similar to the treatment of fleas. However, you must be quicker to deal with ticks as the damage caused by them is much greater. Ticks tend to harpoon which means that they dig deep into the skin of the dog to drink the blood. In that process, they also cause diseases like Rocky Mountain Disease, Lynn disease and tick bite paralysis that are severe and difficult to treat.

• Mites: There are several types of mites that vary in the kind of proboscis or mouth that they have. The best way to keep your dog free from mites is to ensure complete hygiene of your dog. Mites may affect several parts of your dog's body including the skin and the ears. The treatment for the mites depends upon the type of mite and the area that it has infested.

Endoparasites:

These are parasites that live inside your English Mastiff and may cause serious internal damage if not treated immediately. The common internal parasites include:

• Roundworms: These parasites live in the intestines of the dog and are known for shedding many eggs. The biggest issue with round worms is that they also infect humans when they come in contact with them. These parasites cause coughing, vomiting and also bloating in puppies. In younger English Mastiffs, roundworms are usually transmitted through the dam's milk. In adults dogs, contact with feces and also rodents causes roundworm infection.

• Hookworms: There are several species of hookworms that are known to infect dogs. The most dangerous ones are usually found in the warmer regions of the world. Some of them may cause a lot of blood loss for your English Mastiff. The only saving grace with these parasites is that they can be treated effectively. When you notice common symptoms like dark stool, weight loss, anemia and also skin problems, have your dog checked for hookworms immediately.

• Tapeworms: Tapeworms are always transmitted by fleas in dogs. While these parasites are not really dangerous for the dogs, they can cause serious damage to us humans. It is possible that the fleas on your dog's fur enter your body through food or through your hands. Then, they release the tapeworms in your body and can cause diseases like alveolar hydatid.

- Heartworms: These parasites are extremely thin and can grow up to 12 inches in length. These worms live in the dog's heart and affect all the blood vessels and surrounding organs. These worms are transmitted to the dog through mosquitoes. If heartworms are not eliminated, your dog might become anemic. The most obvious symptoms of heart worm infection include fatigue, coughing and lack of appetite.

Ophthalmic Diseases

Dogs are prone to several eye related issues that need to be taken care of at the earliest. Just like humans, the eyes play a vital role in the cognitive functioning of a dog. Any abnormality or problem related to the vision of your pet requires immediate attention and effective treatment for your dog to be active and remain at the pink of his health.

There is no single cause for eye related issues. However, there are some causal factors that are common for all breeds of dogs. Any injury such as a cat scratch is the primary reason for infections and visual issues in dogs. Some infections like conjunctivitis may be caused by bacterial, viral or fungal infections. Such infections might be offshoots of systemic infections or might be localized to the eyes of your English Mastiff.

In case of the English Mastiff, all the common eye problems including eye lid conformation problems, glaucoma and retinal degeneration are genetic in origin. Therefore, when you purchase a puppy, make sure that both the parents have been check thoroughly by a veterinary ophthalmologist and certified eye disease free. These genetic diseases are easily detected when your English Mastiff is a puppy. Therefore, have him checked thoroughly by a vet before you bring him home.

4. Dental Care for Your English Mastiff

Studies show that at least 50% of dogs have some form of gum disease by the time they are three years old. This must be avoided as dental problems are not localized in dogs. When there is tartar or plaque buildup on the teeth, the bacteria that thrive also enter the blood stream of the English Mastiff. Some of these bacteria may cause serious damage to the vital organs of your English Mastiff.

Therefore, a routine dental check up is mandatory. They first and most important dental visit is when your English Mastiff is six months old. This is when the dentist will be able to confirm that your English Mastiff has teeth that are fully developed and in good condition. After this, you must fix a schedule for routine check up and dental maintenance for your English Mastiff.

In order to avoid issues like mouth odor and plaque make sure that your brush your English Mastiff's mouth regularly. However, if you observe problems like hesitation to chew, loss of appetite and bad mouth odor, take your pet to the dentist immediately.

Chapter 15: Behavioral Problems in the English Mastiff

Sometimes your vet may also have to deal with the psychological issues that your English Mastiff faces. The temperament of each dog is formed when he is in his mother's womb. So, we have very little control over that. What we can control, however, is the behavior of the dog. By training him effectively, we can reduce the following behavioral problems:

Aggression

This is a behavioral problem that most pet owners have to deal with. However, when you are dealing with a large dog like the English Mastiff, aggression is actually a problem as it can become potentially dangerous. When a dog becomes aggressive, he tends to attack people and other animals. This behavior is not just inappropriate, it is also hazardous. Therefore, you must never ignore this behavior.

The earliest signs of aggression are lunging and biting. As your dog becomes more aggressive, he will start growling and even bearing his teeth. This is frightening even for the owner. Usually, dogs show aggression as a sign of dominance. So, the first step is to establish the fact that your dog does not have a dominant role in your household. Next, you must determine if the source of aggression is something else. For this, you must observe the behavior of your dog thoroughly.

When you know that your dog is being aggressive, try your best to avoid provoking him. You must silently observe your dog. If he is trying to protect himself as a large animal by putting his chest out and keeping his ears sharp, you must immediately understand that he is trying to assert his dominance. Even if you have the reason for your dog's behavior completely figured out, do not try to solve the issue yourself. An aggressive dog is also unpredictable. Therefore, you need a specialist like a behavioral psychologist to help your English Mastiff. If you are unable to control the aggression of our dog effectively, you may have to send him away as he is a hazard to your family.

Usually, aggression manifests in two forms:

• Aggression towards dogs: An English Mastiff is aggressive towards another dog for two reasons. The first one is if he has not been exposed to other dogs when he was younger. So, he sees another dog as a threat. The other reason is that he is simply trying to assert his dominance.

• Dominant Aggression: English Mastiffs are alpha dogs. This means that they will want to lead a pack in the absence of a good leader. In case of the English Mastiff, your family is his pack. So, if you do not show him right from the beginning that you are the leader, he will try to take over. The best ways to ensure that you are the leader is to establish that you are the source of food and security right from when he is a puppy. The next thing to do is to train him well and train him consistently so that he gets used to receiving commands from you.

Sexual behaviors

Sexual behavior displayed by dogs varies from one individual to another. While some dogs are quite calm even when they are in heat, some of them become overly aggressive when they are ready for the mating season. Usually, in order to curb inappropriate sexual behavior, vets recommend that you have your English Mastiff spayed by the time he is 1 year old. Spaying or Neutering has the following advantages:

- Sexual behavior is not prominent. The dogs are usually calm and less aggressive when they are neutered.
- Since their hormones are in control, dogs are much easier to train when they have been neutered.
- Diseases like cancer of the testicles may be avoided in adult dogs when they are spayed.

Of course, if you want to enroll your English Mastiff in shows or breed your English Mastiff, spaying or
Neutering is not an option. In such cases you must understand the sexual cycle of your English Mastiff. For instance, a female has two estruses each year. Every cycle lasts for 3 weeks. In case a bitch is not mated in this season, she will develop false pregnancy. The mammary gland will become enlarged and she will show maternal affection towards all her toys.

In males, mounting is common when they are not mated in the right season. They will mount on just about anything to relieve their sexual tension. Speak to your breeder in order to avoid this sexual tension from manifesting as aggression.

Jumping

Jumping is a dog's favorite way of greeting his owner. While you may be used to it, having a dog the size of an English Mastiff jump on them might be unnerving to people who are new to him. So, to keep him well behaved at all times, try to curb this habit. Whenever your dog starts jumping use a sharp command like "no" or "off" to tell him that you do not appreciate his enthusiasm. Try to force him to sit as you praise him generously. When he does obey you, pet him and feed him a treat.

Digging

If you come home to find several holes in your yard, you know who has done it! It is your English Mastiff, of course. Now, digging is a habit that is instinctive for dogs. For ages, dogs have made holes to look for food or hide their food. So, although we expect the modern lines to have given up this habit, they are still ardent diggers.

In the modern dogs, however, the reason for digging is quite different. It is a great pastime for when they are bored out of their minds. So, if you give your dog ample exercise, you might be able to help him drop the habit of digging.

Another easy way to control your English Mastiff's digging habit is to provide him with a designated area in your home where he can dig to his heart's fill. It is not right for you to cut off an activity that is so instinctive to him. So, the best thing to do would be to redirect his energy and his habit so that he can develop a healthy habit that fits into your lifestyle too.

Barking

Barking is a behavioral problem only when it is incessant and untimely. Your English Mastiff is using his bark as a way to protect you. So, you must not really stop your English Mastiff from baking altogether. After all, he is a guard dog whose job is to inform you when there is an intruder in your property! So, whether it is a friendly neighbor or an intruder, they are all threats to your English Mastiff and you can expect him to bark. This is his way of warning your and ensuring that you know when danger is impending.

So, when does barking become a problem? When your English Mastiff barks for no reason at all! Yes, he will indulge in incessant barking if he is not stopped. All he is trying to do is grab your attention. The best way to solve the issue of barking is by understanding the kinds of barks and the message behind them. For instance, the bark of a dog when he sees a squirrel is very different from when he wants food! When you are able to tell this difference, you will be able to cut down on unwanted barking. A barking issue will become very evident at a really young age. If you tell your dog "no" and reward him when he is calm and quiet, he will learn not to bark unnecessarily.

Food begging

The ultimate goal for any dog is to get his hands on the treats that he sees around your home. Some dogs simply steal the food while some dogs beg for foods from the table. Both these habits are unacceptable are your English Mastiff may get his paws on some food that he is allergic to. There are also some foods like candy that are not good for the dogs and must be avoided at all times.

At a very young age, dogs form this notion that their masters are keeping all the good food for themselves. So they will try every tactic possible to get some of the good food. The habit of begging is triggered by specific stimuli. For instance, when your dog hears the sound of cutlery or dishes just before you sit down to eat, he will stand with his paws in the air, wag his tail and look at your intently for some food.

The only way to curb this habit is by ignoring him. Dogs are clever creatures and will try to whine and cry to guilt you into giving them food. You must ignore the habit as much as you can till it becomes extinct. Instruct all your family members to do the same and discourage bad behavior.

Dealing with Behavioral Problems

In order to curb behavioral problems, here are some simple tips that you can follow:

- Never reprimand or punish a dog for wrong behavior.
- Observe his behavior carefully.
- If your dog is displaying bad behavior, do not reward him to change the behavior. He will think of the reward as an incentive for displaying the bad habit. For instance, a dog will be quiet when he is given a treat if he is barking. This

however makes your dog thing that he is being rewarded for barking
- Take the help of a behavioral specialist
- Be extremely patient while dealing with a dog's behavioral problems.

Training from an early age is the only sure shot way of ensuring that your dog is well mannered and well behaved.

Chapter 16: Showing an English Mastiff

Showing your dogs in a competition is not just about getting your dog to look good and cute. There are several things that you must do from when your dog is still a puppy. If you have decided that your dog is meant for shows, then training him is crucial. After all, you want your dog to enjoy the process of showing just as much as you and the others present there. Here are some tips to give your dog an advantage over the rest when he is presented at shows:

Socialization is a must!

Showmanship is a very important trait among dogs. If your dog is not socialized at a young age, there is no chance that he will make a good show dog. Even if your English Mastiff is great at conformation, he will not stand out and shine the way he must if he is not comfortable around people. Each time you take the dog to a new place, he will be unable to perform well as his shyness overpowers his skills. To socialize your dog:

- Take him wherever you go after he has been vaccinated as a puppy.
- Make him aware of various environments. He must be exposed to different surfaces like cement, wood, grass, carpet, rubber etc.
- Take him to new places and allow him to meet new people.
- There are several puppy kindergartens that you can take your English Mastiff to. These classes are meant to help your English Mastiff socialize with several other dogs and puppies.
- Do not stop people from petting and interacting with your puppy. When he is young, your English Mastiff will be more allowing of this than when he is grown up.

191

Socialization builds confidence in dogs. This is a winning quality that all judges love! Any dog who is comfortable being around people will be able to display all his tricks confidently and will therefore be loved by the crowd as well as all those on the panel.

Attend conformation classes

There are several kennels and clubs that have weekly classes that are directed towards training your dog for conformation. You can enroll yourself and your dog into these classes. These classes are usually conducted by dog handlers who have immense experience with show dogs. If you are a novice in exhibiting, these classes are mandatory for you. You will learn all the basics of showing your dog in a ring. It is also a great way to train your dog to understand what is expected of him when he is a show dog. In these classes, you will learn things like:

• Walking your dog around the ring. This is known as gaiting in show terms.
• Stacking the dog on a table or on the ground for the examination. For a large dog like the English Mastiff, stacking is usually done on the ground.
• Helping your dog perform basic patterns like down, back, the L, the triangle etc.

Not all dogs are meant to be show dogs. In case your English Mastiff is not among the 'show ring' dogs, you must understand that you are putting a lot of unnecessary pressure on him. When you attend a conformation class, you will be able to seek professional help to decide whether your dog really belongs in the ring or not.

Keep your dog well groomed

The last thing the judges want to see in the ring is a shabby dog. You must make sure that your English Mastiff is completely clean before he enters the show ring. This means, he must be bathed, combed and free from fleas. Some spot cleaning might be necessary for a dog who is going into the ring. For this, you get several powders and sprays that act as dry soaps to keep your dog clean. You must try to time your dog's bath close to the show dates. Although it is not recommended to give most dogs a weekly bath, you must at least have him thoroughly cleaned before a show. If you choose to spot bathe him, focus on areas like the face, the undercarriage and his legs.

Trimming

For most Mastiffs, trimming the fur on the entire body is not a necessity. However, you may have to 'sculpt' the fur of your dog to ensure that he looks neat and clean for the judges. This makes your dog visually appealing and influences what a judge sees on the outside. Here are some trimming tips for your English Mastiff:

- If you feel like his legs are too close together, you can trim the fur around the paws. This gives your dog a good stance by making his paws seem well apart from each other.
- If the excess hair on the head, chin, tail and ears is cut off, a dog looks more youthful. This can be included in your regular grooming sessions.
- There is always a small amount of hair that is present directly in front of the tail. Trimming this hair makes it seem like your dog's tail is placed slightly higher.

Never start first or enter last

When you finally make it to the show ring, your timing is very important. Starting off right in the beginning or entering the ring last is never a good idea. If you have a choice when it comes to your position, try to enter in the middle. This gives you a few advantages:

- You can stack your dog well for exhibition. Last minute cleaning, brushing etc. can be taken care of. If you are first in line, you will be up for examination immediately after you have finished gaiting around the ring.

• If you are the last handler, you will have very little time for a touch up. After examining the dogs thoroughly, the judges usually give the dogs one last look that is the deciding factor.

Watch the judge

Watching your judge will give you the advantage of time. It will also make you seem more professional in you approach. When you keep an eye on the judge, you will be able to tell exactly what he is doing in the ring. That way, there is no chance that your dog's faults are revealed to the judge as you are always alert. When the judge calls you up, you will be able to enter immediately if you are watching. Wasting a judge's time is a bad idea as it reduces the time that your dog gets for the exhibition.

Understand the right gait speed

Perfect conformation is a rarity among dogs. Every dog has a slight fault that you must be aware of as the parent. Usually the problem is in the gait of the dog. It is possible to cover or camouflage this fault by understanding the right pace at which the dog must be gaited. Choose a speed that allows your dog to walk at his best. To understand the right speed you need to watch his normal gait. Observe the hind legs when he is walking away from you. If you notice that his legs seem week or that the hocks are leaning towards one another, you can try to walk the dog faster or slower to get a better gait. Similarly watch the front legs. If you notice that his feet converge, you need to adjust the pace to make it better. When you look at the dog from the side, you should not see the shoulders hunched. They must be relaxed. Also the feet must not kick out. The top line should not bounce up and down. When you have achieved all this, you can safely say that your dog has a good gait.

The last thing to do is stay calm. Just make sure that your dog is between you and the judge whenever you are showing him. That way you are not in the way of the judge. You must try to keep yourself calm at all times. Dogs are extremely sensitive to your feelings. If there is any sense of doubt or anxiety in your touch, your dog will feel it instantly and will feel less confident.

Once your dog has been trained to do his job, he will do it properly. The idea is to just enjoy the experience of working with your dog as a team. As long as you are focused on that, you have no reason to worry during a show!

Chapter 17: Cost of Owning an English Mastiff

When you bring home an English Mastiff, you must be prepared to take on the financial commitments. Here is a list of expenses that you will have to bear when you decide to bring an English Mastiff home.

The dog: $2000- $4000/ £1000- 2000

Council registration: $50- 150/ £25- 75

Neutering: $200/ £100

Pet insurance: $60 per month or £30 per month

Micro chipping: $50/ £30

Vaccinations: $50-$70/ £20-£50

Crate: $30-$50/ £15-30

Toys: $30/ £15 for basics

Ongoing Costs

Food: $60-100/ £30-90 per week

Worming medications: $2.50/ £1.50 per week

Vaccination Boosters: $18 - 25/ £10-12 per shot

Veterinary checks: $100-250/ £50-120 per annum

Pet sitter: $10- 25/ £5-10 per day

It can be difficult to accurately estimate what the cost of owning every dog might be because there are too many variables and unexpected medical problems, which might arise that may not otherwise be considered average.

For instance, you may like to buy new collars and leashes every year, the latest toys and gadgets, or the most expensive food for your dog every week that might also not be considered average. However, when thinking about sharing your life with a dog, it's important to consider more than just the daily cost of feeding your dog.

Many humans do not think about whether or not they can truly afford to care for a dog before they bring one home, and not being prepared can cause stress and problems later on. Remember that being financially responsible for your dog is a large part of being a good guardian. Beyond the initial investment of purchasing your puppy from a reputable breeder, for most guardians, owning a dog will include the costs associated with the following:

Food
Treats
Pee pads, poop bags, potty patches
Leashes and collars
Safety harnesses
Travel kennels or bags
House training pens
Clothing
Toys
Beds
Professional grooming or equipment
Shampoo and conditioner
Neutering or spaying
Regular veterinary care
Obedience or dog whispering classes
Pet sitting, walking or boarding
Pet insurance

Tattooing
Micro-chipping
Yearly licensing
Unexpected emergencies

As you can see from the list above, there are many variables involved with being a canine guardian that may or may not apply to your particular situation. For instance, depending upon where you shop, what type of food and how much you feed your dog, what sort of veterinarian or grooming care you choose, whether or not you have pet insurance and what types of items you purchase for your dog's well being, the yearly cost of owning a dog could be estimated at anywhere between $700 and $3,000 (£420 and £1,800) per year. Other contributing factors that may have an effect on the overall yearly cost of owning a dog can include the region where you live, the weather, the accessibility of the items you need, your own lifestyle preferences and your dog's age and individual needs.

NOTE: another interesting fact that may influence the overall cost associated with caring for a particular breed of dog is, according to a recent study of 2,000 dogs, closely related to what breed of dog you may be sharing your home with.

According to a recent article written by Sarah Griffiths and published in the Daily Mail on June 13, 2014, there is now a list of the top ten most *"destructive"* purebred dog breeds. This interesting study was carried out in reference to damage a dog may cause by ripping up the carpet, chewing through the fence, destroying the plants in the garden, eating the remote or your most expensive shoes, etc. Of course, all us humans expect some degree of damage from our furry friends during their lifetime, however, sometimes it can be quite a surprisingly large amount when you begin to add up the total amounts spent on cleaning, replacing and repairing damaged property, and the amount can be even higher if your dog becomes involved in destroying the neighbor's property, too.

The prize for the top ten destroyer is awarded to the cute and tiny Chihuahua, with average repair costs totaling $1,468. (£866) over the dog's lifetime, followed by the Dachshund, Dalmatian, Bulldog, Great Dane, Husky, Beagle, Pointer and German Shepherd. On the other hand, the top ten least destructive breeds include the Staffordshire Bull Terrier, causing a reported $302. (£178) worth of damage over the dog's lifetime, followed by the West Highland White Terrier, Yorkshire Terrier, Spaniel, Whippet, Shih Tzu, Labrador, Jack Russell, Rottweiler and Sheepdog.

NOTE: the more popular a particular breed may be, and the more positive traits a particular breed may enjoy will also make the cost of initially purchasing a puppy from a breeder more costly

Chapter 18: Caring for Aging Dogs

1. What to Be Aware Of

As a result of many modern advances in veterinarian care, improvements in diet and nutrition and general knowledge concerning proper care of our canine companions, our dogs are able to enjoy longer, healthier lives. As such, when caring for our canine companions, we need to be aware of behavioral and physical changes that will affect our dogs as they approach old age.

a) Physiological Changes
As our beloved canine companions enter into their senior years, they may be suffering from very similar, physical aging problems that affect us humans, such as pain, stiffness and arthritis, and inability to control their bowels and bladder. Any of these problems will reduce a dog's willingness to want to exercise.

b) Behavioral Changes
Further, a senior dog may experience behavioral changes resulting from loss of hearing and sight, such as disorientation, fear or startle reactions and overall grumpiness from any number of physical problems that could be causing them pain whenever they move. Just as research and science has improved our human quality of life in our senior years, the same is becoming true for our canine counterparts who are able to benefit from dietary supplements and pharmaceutical products to help them be as comfortable as possible in their senior years. Of course, there will be some inconveniences associated with keeping a dog with advancing years around the home, however, your dog deserves no

less than to spend their final days in your loving care after they have unconditionally given you their entire lives.

c) Geriatric Dogs

Being aware of the changes that are likely occurring in a senior dog will help you to better care for them during their geriatric years. For instance, most dogs will experience hearing loss and visual impairment, and how you help them will depend upon which goes first (hearing or sight). For instance, if a dog's hearing is compromised, then using more hand signals will be helpful. This is also another good reason to teach your dog hand signals when they are young so you can still communicate with your dog when he is a senior and when he is deaf.

Deaf dogs will still be able to hear louder noises and feel vibrations, therefore hand clapping, knocking on walls, doors or furniture, using a loud clicker or stomping your foot on the floor may be a way to get their attention. If a senior dog loses their eyesight, most dogs will still be able to easily navigate their familiar surroundings, and you will only need to be extra watchful on their behalf when taking them to unfamiliar territory.

If they still have their hearing, you will be able to assist your dog with verbal cues and commands. Dogs that have lost both their hearing and their sight will need to be close to you so that they can relax and not feel nervous, and so that you can communicate by touching parts of their body.

Generally speaking, even when a dog becomes blind and/or deaf, their powerful sense of smell is still functioning, which means that they will be able to smell where you are and navigate their environment by using their nose.

d) More Bathroom Breaks

Bathroom breaks may need to become more frequent in older dogs who may lose their ability to hold it for longer periods of time, so be prepared to be more watchful and to offer them opportunities to go outside more frequently during the day. You may also want to place a pee pad near the door, in case they just can't hold it long enough, or if you have not already taught them to bathroom on an indoor potty patch, or pee pad, now may be the time for this alternative bathroom arrangement. A dog who has been house trained for years will feel the shame and upset of not being able to hold it long enough to get to their regular bathroom location, so be kind and do whatever you need to do in order to help them not to have to feel bad about failing bowel or bladder control.

Our beloved canine companions may also begin to show signs of cognitive decline and changes in the way their brain functions, similar to what happens to humans suffering from Alzheimer's, where they start to wander about aimlessly, sometimes during the middle of the night. Make sure that if this is happening with your dog at nighttime, that they cannot accidentally fall down stairs or harm themselves in any way.

Being aware that an aging dog will be experiencing many symptoms that are similar to an aging human will help you to understand how best to keep them safe and as comfortable as possible during this golden time in their lives.

2. How to Make Them Comfortable

a) Regular Checkups
During this time in your dog's life, when their immune systems become weakened and they may be experiencing pain, you will want to get into the habit of taking your senior dog for regular veterinarian checkups. Take them for a checkup every six months so that early detection of any problems can quickly be attended to and solutions for helping to keep your aging dog comfortable can be provided.

b) No Rough Play
An older dog will not have the same energy or willingness to play that they did when they were younger, therefore, do not allow younger children to rough house with an older dog. Explain to

them that the dog is getting older and that as a result they must learn to be gentle and to leave the dog alone when it may want to rest or sleep.

c) Mild Exercise

Dogs still love going for walks, even when they are getting older and slowing down. Although an older dog will generally have less energy, they still need to exercise and keep moving, and taking them out regularly for shorter or slower walks will keep them healthier and happier long into old age.

d) Best Quality Food

Everyone has heard the saying, *"you are what you eat"* and for a senior dog, what he or she eats is even more important as his or her digestive system may no longer be functioning at peak performance. Therefore, feeding a high quality, protein-based food will be important for a senior dog's continued health.

As well, if your older dog is overweight, you will want to help them shed excess pounds so that they will not be placing undue stress on their joints or heart. The best way to accomplish this is by feeding smaller quantities of a higher quality food.

e) Clean and Parasite Free

The last thing an aging dog should have to deal with is the misery of itching and scratching, so make sure that you continue to give them regular baths with the appropriate shampoos and conditioners to keep their coat and skin comfortable and free from biting bugs.

f) Plenty of Water

Proper hydration is essential for helping to keep an older dog comfortable. Water is life giving for every creature, so make certain that your aging dog has easy access to plenty of clean, fresh water which will help to improve their energy and digestion and also prevent dehydration which can add to joint stiffness.

g) Keep Them Warm

Just as older humans feel the cold more, so do older dogs. Keeping your senior warm will help to alleviate some of the pain of their joint stiffness or arthritis. Make sure their bed or kennel is not kept in a drafty location and perhaps consider a heated bed for them. Be aware that your aging dog will be more sensitive to extremes in temperature, and it will be up to you to make sure that they are comfortable at all times, which means not too hot and not too cold.

h) Indoor Clothing

We humans tend to wear warmer clothing as we get older, simply because we have more difficulty maintaining a comfortable body temperature and the same will be true of our senior companions. Therefore, while you most likely already have a selection of outdoor clothing appropriate to the climate in which you live, you may not have considered keeping your dog warm while inside the home. Now would be the time to consider doggy t-shirts or sweater clothing options to help keep your aging companion comfortably warm both inside and out.

i) Steps or Stairs

If your dog is allowed to sleep on the human couch or chair, but they are having difficulties getting up there as their joints are becoming stiff and painful, consider buying or making them a set of soft, foam stairs so that they do not have to make the jump to their favorite sleeping place.

j) Comfortable Bed

While most dogs seem to be happy with sleeping on the floor, providing a padded, soft bed will greatly help to relieve sore spots and joint pain in older dogs.

If there is a draft in the home, generally it will be at floor level, therefore, a bed that is raised up off of the floor will be warmer for your senior.

k) More Love and Attention

Last, but not least, make sure that you give your senior lots of love and attention and never leave them alone for long periods of time. When they are not feeling their best, they will want to be with you all that much more because you are their trusted guardian whom they love beyond life itself.

3. What is Euthanasia?

Every veterinarian will have received special training to help provide all incurably ill, injured or aged pets that have come to the end of their natural lives with a humane and gentle death, through a process called *"euthanasia"*. When the time comes, euthanasia, or putting a dog *"to sleep"*, will usually be a two-step process.

First, the veterinarian will inject the dog with a sedative to make them sleepy, calm and comfortable. Second, the veterinarian will inject a special drug that will peacefully stop their heart.

These drugs work in such a way that the dog will not experience any awareness whatsoever that their life is ending. What they will experience is very much like what we humans experience when falling asleep under anesthesia during a surgical procedure. Once the second stage drug has been injected, the entire process takes about 10 to 20 seconds, at which time the veterinarian will then check to make certain that the dog's heart has stopped.

There is no suffering with this process, which is a very gentle and humane way to end a dog's suffering and allow them to peacefully pass on.

4. When to Help a Dog Transition

The impending loss of a beloved dog is one of the most painfully difficult and emotionally devastating experiences a canine guardian will ever have to face. For the sake of our faithful companions, because we do not want to prolong their suffering, we humans will have to do our best to look at our dog's situation practically, rather than emotionally, so that we can make the best decision for them.

They may be suffering from extreme old age and the inability to even walk outside to relieve themselves, and thus having to deal with the indignity of regularly soiling their sleeping area, they may have been diagnosed with an incurable illness that is causing them much pain, or they may have been seriously injured. Whatever the reason for a canine companions suffering, it will be up to their human guardian to calmly guide the end-of-life experience so that any further discomfort and distress can be minimized.

What to Do If You Are Uncertain

In circumstances where it is not entirely clear how much a dog is suffering, it will be helpful to pay close attention to your dog's behavior and keep a daily log or record so that you can know for certain how much of their day is difficult and painful for them, and how much is not. When you keep a daily log, it will be easier to decide if the dog's quality of life has become so poor that it makes better sense to offer them the gift of peacefully going to sleep.

During this time of uncertainty, it will also be very important to discuss with your veterinarian what signs of suffering may be associated with the dog's particular disease or condition, so that you know what to look for. Often a dog may still continue to eat or drink despite being upset, having difficulty breathing, excessively panting, being disoriented or in much pain, and as their caring guardians, we will have to weigh their love of eating against how much they are really suffering in all other aspects of their life.

Obviously, if a canine guardian can clearly see that their beloved companion is suffering throughout their days and nights, it will make sense to help humanely end their suffering by planning a euthanasia procedure. We humans are often tempted to delay the inevitable moment of euthanasia, because we love our dogs so much and cannot bear the anticipation of the intense grief we know will overwhelm us when we must say our final goodbyes to our beloved fur friend. Unfortunately, we may regret that we allowed our dog to suffer too long, and could find ourselves wishing that if only we humans had the same option, to peacefully let go, when we find ourselves in such a stage in our own lives.

5. Grieving a Lost Pet

Some humans do not fully recognize the terrible grief involved in losing a beloved canine friend. There will be many who do not understand the close bond we humans can have with our dogs, which is often unlike any we have with our human counterparts.

Your friends may give you pitying looks and try to cheer you up, but if they have never experienced such a loss themselves, they may also secretly think that you are making too much fuss over "just a dog". For some of us humans, the loss of a beloved dog is so painful that we decide never to share our lives with another, because we cannot bear the thought of going through the pain of loss again. Expect to feel terribly sad, tearful and yes, depressed because those who are close to their canine companions will feel their loss no less acutely than the loss of a human friend or life partner.

The grieving process can take some time to recover from, and some of us never totally recover. After the loss of a family dog, first you need to take care of yourself by making certain that you keep eating and getting regular sleep, even though you will feel an almost eerie sense of loneliness.

Losing a beloved dog is a shock to the system, which can also affect your concentration and your ability to find joy or want to participate in other activities that may be part of your daily life. During this early grieving time you will need to take extra care while driving or performing tasks that require your concentration as you may find yourself distracted.

If there are other dogs or pets in the home, they will also be grieving the loss of a companion, and may display this by acting depressed, being off their food or showing little interest in play or games. Therefore, you need to help guide your other pets through this grieving process by keeping them busy and interested, taking them for extra walks and spending more time with them. Many people do not wait long enough before attempting to replace a lost pet and will immediately go to the local shelter and rescue a deserving dog. While this may help to distract you from your grieving process, this is not really fair to the new fur member of your family.

Bringing a new pet into a home that is depressed and grieving the loss of a long time canine member may create behavioral problems for the new dog who will be faced with learning all about their new home while also dealing with the unstable, sad energy of the grieving family. A better scenario would be to allow yourself the time to properly grieve by waiting a minimum of one month to allow yourself and your family to feel happier and more stable before deciding upon sharing your home with another dog.

The grieving process will be different for everyone and you will know when the time is right to consider sharing your home with another canine companion.

6. The Rainbow Bridge Poem

"Just this side of heaven is a place called Rainbow Bridge.

When an animal dies that has been
especially close to someone here,
that pet goes to Rainbow Bridge.
There are meadows and hills for all of our special friends
so they can run and play together.

There is plenty of food, water and sunshine,
and our friends are warm and comfortable.

All the animals who had been ill and old
are restored to health and vigor;
those who were hurt or maimed
are made whole and strong again,
just as we remember them in our dreams
of days and times gone by.
The animals are happy and content,
except for one small thing;
they each miss someone very special to them,
who had to be left behind.

They all run and play together,
but the day comes when one suddenly stops
and looks into the distance.
His bright eyes are intent; His eager body quivers.
Suddenly he begins to run from the group,
flying over the green grass,
his legs carrying him faster and faster.

You have been spotted,
and when you and your special friend finally meet,
you cling together in joyous reunion,
never to be parted again.
The happy kisses rain upon your face;
your hands again caress the beloved head,
and you look once more into the trusting eyes
of your pet, so long gone from your life
but never absent from your heart.

Then you cross Rainbow Bridge together...."
www.rainbowbridge.com

- Author unknown

Conclusion

Getting a pet home is a real commitment. Unless you are entirely ready, think about it, discuss it with your family and then bring your English Mastiff home.

In the end, the most important thing to know is whether an English Mastiff is the right dog for you or not. There are some obvious things that will help you make this vital decision. Here is a list of pros and cons of having an English Mastiff in your home:

Pros:

- They are great companions
- They are the best work dogs
- Grooming needs are not many
- They are even tempered
- They are good for homes with children and other pets
- They are loyal and protective
- They are easy to train
- They are excellent show dogs

Cons:

- May be dangerous if not trained well
- They are really large
- They are not suitable for first time owners
- Highly attention seeking
- Expensive to maintain
- They need a single master to command them

210

- Dominant by nature

Once you have considered these pros and cons, you may step right up to a breeder and bring home your gorgeous English Mastiff. I do hope that this book has been adequate in providing you with all the information you need about the English Mastiff. All the research for this book is based on personal accounts and insights by experts who have a great deal of experience with the English Mastiff. I hope you enjoyed this book.

Published by IMB Publishing 2014

Made in the USA
San Bernardino, CA
14 October 2015